W9-DIE-251

Excavations at Seila, Egypt

RELIGIOUS STUDIES CENTER PUBLICATIONS

BOOK OF MORMON SYMPOSIUM SERIES

The Book of Mormon: The
Keystone Scripture

The Book of Mormon: First
Nephi, the Doctrinal
Foundation

MONOGRAPH SERIES

Nibley on the Timely and the
Timeless
Reflections on Mormonism
Literature of Belief
The Words of Joseph Smith
Book of Mormon Authorship
Mormons and Muslims

Isaiah and the Prophets
Scriptures for the Modern World
The Joseph Smith Translation:
The Restoration of Plain and
Precious Things
Apocryphal Writings and the
Latter-Day Saints

SPECIALIZED MONOGRAPH SERIES

Supporting Saints: Life Stories
of Nineteenth-Century
Mormons
The Call of Zion: The Story of
the First Welsh Mormon
Emigration

The Religion and Family
Connection: Social Science
Perspectives
Welsh Mormon Writings
from 1844 to 1862:
A Historical Bibliography

Excavations at Seila, Egypt

Edited with an Introduction by
C. Wilfred Griggs

Volume One
Occasional Papers
of the
Religious Studies Center

Religious Studies Center
Brigham Young University
Provo, Utah

Copyright © 1988 by
Religious Studies Center
Brigham Young University

All rights reserved

Library of Congress Catalog Card Number: 88-72066
ISBN 0-88494-647-9

First Printing, 1988

Produced and Distributed by
BOOKCRAFT, INC.
Salt Lake City, Utah

Printed in the United States of America

RELIGIOUS STUDIES CENTER
BRIGHAM YOUNG UNIVERSITY

General Director: Robert J. Matthews
Associate General Director: Donald Q. Cannon
Assistant General Director (Publications): Charles D. Tate, Jr.

Area Directors

Ancient Studies:	C. Wilfred Griggs
Bible:	Victor L. Ludlow
Book of Mormon:	Monte S. Nyman
Church History:	Larry C. Porter
Doctrine and Covenants:	Larry E. Dahl
Pearl of Great Price:	H. Donl Peterson
Special Projects:	John W. Welch

Advisory Board

Robert J. Matthews
Stan L. Albrecht
Todd A. Britsch

Contents

Contents

Preface

The Religious Studies Center inaugurates its *Occasional Papers* series with the preliminary reports from the 1984 field campaign of the Brigham Young University excavation team at Seila in the Fayum in Egypt. As both this set of reports and those expected from later expeditions will demonstrate, the work done near the Egyptian town of Seila will have a significant impact on further studies of not only Egypt's Old Kingdom but also the Greco-Roman era.

The unique strength of the BYU excavation team is that it is composed of men representing many different disciplines. The essays in this volume demonstrate the unusually broad approach to the project this diversity of specialists allowed the team to take. Whereas most excavations are directed by one or two archaeologists who take recovered artifacts and data from the site to the experts, the BYU project is noteworthy for taking the specialists to the site, where each can work not only with materials relating to his interest but also within the context of others doing the same in their own disciplines. Enhanced perspectives, interdisciplinary observations from several different perspectives at the site combine to make the BYU team's approach to excavating an unusually effective one.

The essays in this volume represent the first season of this interdisciplinary team effort at Seila, Egypt. It is to be understood that they are tentative, exploratory studies which are subject to alteration as more information comes to light from subsequent field seasons and from work of other investigators. Later reports will involve yet other areas of specialization such as textile analysis, metallurgy, botany, and hair studies, to name just a few.

The views expressed in these papers are the authors' own and do not necessarily reflect those of The Church of Jesus Christ of Latter-day Saints, Brigham Young University, or the Religious Studies Center.

S. KENT BROWN AND CHARLES D. TATE, JR.

Introduction

Few academic disciplines conjure up as many romantic scenes and expectations as archaeology, and no country has had a more spellbinding effect on western civilization during the past two and one half millennia than Egypt. From the fifth century B.C., when the Greek historian Herodotus devoted one book of his history to Egypt (although the subject of his work was the Greek-Persian wars), to the discovery in the twentieth century of the tomb and treasures of Tutankhamen, fascination with the ancient civilization of the Nile valley has never ceased. Less well-known than Herodotus or Howard Carter, but not less important in the reconstruction of the history of Egypt, are the ongoing historical and archaeological efforts of teams of scholars from around the world. The glamor, danger, and excitement of such work are far removed from the "Hollywood" depictions in recent movie films, but one cannot overlook the expectation and thrill of discovering an artifact which sheds greater understanding on the life, religion, livelihood, and accomplishments of people who lived thousands of years ago. No less exciting are the clues from the earth itself relating to the formation and geological changes which a site has undergone over much greater periods of time. The collected essays in this volume deal with both the geology and history of an unusually interesting site in Egypt, located on the eastern edge of the Fayum depression, or due west from the Meidum pyramid if one is taking his bearings from the Nile valley.

Since the late 1970's, Professor Leonard Lesko, then the senior Egyptologist at the University of California, Berkeley, and Professor C. Wilfred Griggs of Brigham Young University (a former student of Dr. Lesko) had discussed the possibility of a joint excavation in Egypt. The opportunity to excavate near the village of Seila, an archaeological site which contains two large cemeteries and a small Old Kingdom pyramid, arose during the display of the Tutankhamen treasures in San Francisco. Dr. Lesko became the project director, Dr. Griggs was the field director, and the project was jointly sponsored by UC Berkeley and BYU. The first season, from January to March, 1981, was divided between the north cemetery, a site named Fag el-Gamous, and the Seila pyramid. A few squares were excavated in the cemetery—not all completely—and the pyramid was partially cleared, with work at both areas of the site showing promise for future seasons.

Altered circumstances, including Dr. Lesko's appointment to an endowed chair of Egyptology at Brown University, led the Egyptian Antiquities Organization (EAO) to invite Dr. Griggs to become the project director of the Seila excavation, and Brigham Young University became the sole sponsoring institution. A small team comprised of Wilfred Griggs, Revell Phillips, and George Homsey went to Egypt in 1983 to survey the site for detailed mapping and to make a preliminary geological analysis. This was followed by a full-scale excavation at the north cemetery in January–March, 1984, with the same staff members plus Mrs. LaRue Phillips, pathologists Dr. Vincent Wood, Dr. Douglas Wyler, and Dr. Eugene Pocock. Two students, Russell Hamblin, a graduate student in the Geology Department at BYU, and Morgan Tanner, an undergraduate archaeology major, were also members of the 1984 team. Professor Keith Rigby of the BYU Geology Department was on site for a brief time, in part to advise Russ Hamblin in his Master's thesis on the geology of the site. The essays in this collection are there ports of activities carried out in the 1984 season. Future seasons will undoubtedly provide data which will expand, limit, or modify the conclusions in these essays, but the participants feel the necessity to make available to interested readers the data of "progressive reports," rather than to wait for a single, final publication.

The inspector assigned by the EAO to work on the site with the team in 1984 was Akram Edward Eshat, and the success of the season was enhanced by his enthusiastic and capable assistance. The team also benefited from the support of Mr. Ali el-Bazidi, chief inspector for the Fayum, as well as Mr. Mostafa el-Zairy, the area director for the general region. Mr. Sabri Gabbour, director of the Kom

Aushim Museum, assisted in making local arrangements for the staff, both for living quarters and numerous other matters. Dr. Ali el-Kholy, director-general of Antiquities for Middle Egypt, gave inestimable help to the project, providing guidance and counsel in many ways. Dr. Ahmed Kadry, director of the EAO, also provided the necessary leadership to see that contracts, security clearances, and like necessities were prepared and in order so that the project could proceed. There were others, too numerous to mention here, whose dedication to the recovery and restoration of Egyptian antiquities is a labor of love, to whom gratitude for the success of the 1984 excavation season is due. It is a pleasure to acknowledge the ongoing friendship and assistance of Dr. Fattah Sabbahy, senior official in the EAO, in the continuation of this project. Grateful acknowledgement is also extended to BYU and its administrators, especially Dr. Jae R. Ballif, Provost and Academic Vice President, for unfailing and unstinting support to this project.

C. WILFRED GRIGGS

(A glossary of terms and abbreviations has been supplied for the non-scientific reader. Eds.)

Ancient Civilizations and Geology of the Eastern Mediterranean

1

Wm. Revell Phillips

The Geologic History

World climate zones are a consequence of persistent cyclic currents in the atmosphere of the earth and have persisted throughout at least the later eras of geologic time. Air warmed by the sun rises near the earth's equator to form the equatorial low and is cooled in the upper troposphere, causing its water content to condense as torrential rains. This warm-humid zone forms a jungle belt about 30 degrees broad centered on the equator. North of this humid jungle zone, winds blow south to the equatorial low from the high pressure at the horse latitudes (30 degrees – 35 degrees). These trade winds blow to the southwest (coriolis effect) and are warmed as they approach the equatorial regions. Warming increases the ability of the air to hold moisture and little rain falls between 15 degrees and 35 degrees north (or south) latitude so that desert zones flank the equatorial jungles. Between the horse latitude high (30 degrees – 35 degrees) and the subpolar low (60 degrees) the prevailing westerlies blow to the northeast and

Wm. Revell Phillips is professor of geology at Brigham Young University.

cool as they approach the polar regions. This temperate climate zone, characterized by periodic, widely distributed rainfall controlled by local topographic features, forms the major agricultural regions of the world, and accommodates most of the world's population.

In the early Mesozoic (c. 200 MYBP) the continental masses of the earth appear to have been clustered as a single land mass (Pangea), largely in the southern hemisphere. A large arm of the single ocean nearly divided a northern land mass (Laurasia) from a southern one (Gondwanaland) as an east-west sea (Tethys Sea) open to the east. Throughout the Mesozoic era the land masses appear to have moved northward; and the Mesozoic sediments of Europe, Asia and North America which began in the humid coal swamps of a tropical jungle and ended in the massive crossbedded sands of a vast desert, indicating the passage of the northern continents through the climate zones described above. The earliest Mesozoic sediments on parts of Africa, South America, India and Australia are of glacial origin, suggesting a cluster of these continents near the south pole.

A plate subduction zone along the northern edge of the Tethys Sea consumed the ocean crust of the Tethys beneath the Laurasian land mass as the southern land mass moved rapidly northward. Small land masses (e.g. Anatolia, Iran, Tibet) riding on the subducting plate impacted on the southern edge of Laurasia, folding on their northern edge the sediments deposited on the continental slopes of Laurasia, and active subduction moved south of these land masses which were now sutured to the northern continent.

In the late Mesozoic (c. 100 MYBP), continental rifting separated the Americas from Europe and Africa and the first ocean crust of the new Atlantic ocean formed along the mid-Atlantic rift. Africa continued its northeast movement against the southern edge of the Eurasian continent further closing the Tethys Sea. A small Italian plate, either as an independent microcontinent or as a northern peninsula on the African plate, impacted against the southern edge of Europe, folding the Tethys sediments and ocean crust into a high mountain range (Alps) and swinging counterclockwise toward the Dalmatian coast (fig. 1).

Figure 1.   Crustal Plates and Plate Motion in the Mediterranean.
The north part of the figure is the Eurasian plate. All motions are
shown by arrows and are relative to the Eurasian plate. The principal
motion is the northward movement of the large African plate (bottom
part of the figure) against the "stationary" Eurasian plate (top part of
the figure). Four smaller plates are caught between and experience
movement largely determined by the behavior of the major plates.
From west to east the minor plates are the Italian, Aegean (or Greek),
Anatolian (or Turkish) and Arabian.

About 50 MYBP (Early Eocene) the Red Sea rift began
to open as the Arabian plate swung counterclockwise away
from Africa to impact on the southern edge of Asia, closing
the old Tethys on the east and forming the Zagros Mountain chain between Arabia and the Iranian Plateau.

The Mediterranean Sea, as a remnant of the ancient
Tethys, was closed on both east and west and diminished
by evaporation in the arid climate of the desert climate
zone. By late Miocene (c. 10 MYBP) the Mediterranean basin
was separated into an eastern and western basin by a ridge
from the Atlas Mountains through Sicily to the Italian Peninsula. The western basin evaporated to complete dryness,
depositing great thicknesses of salt in the Balearic Sea, and
the eastern basin contained little more than an isolated
saline lake thousands of feet below sea level. The major
rivers cut huge, Grand Canyon-like gorges into the sub-sea

3

level Mediterranean basins. The Rhone River was the only major river emptying into the western basin but, in the eastern basin, the Nile emptied waters from the equatorial jungles and, through the Dardanelles and Bosphorous, waters poured from the Black Sea and the rivers of Central Europe and Russia. By early Pliocene (c. 5 MYBP) the Atlantic broke into the arid Mediterranean basin through the Gibraltar Strait and the world's greatest waterfall must have been spectacular for a thousand years as the Mediterranean basin filled to the prevailing sea level. The huge river canyons were flooded and Pliocene sediments were deposited in the Nile gulf and the embayments formed by the other major rivers. The Nile and Rhone refilled their valleys with sediment from the African jungles and western Europe; however, the Dardanelles-Bosphorous still remains a deep waterway allowing the access of deep-water shipping to the Black Sea, perhaps because the Black Sea acts as a catch basin for river sediments, and the short stretch of river from the Black Sea to the Mediterranean carries little sediment.

The level of the Mediterranean was subject to the rise and fall of worldwide sea level with the cyclic growth and decline of continental glaciers throughout the Pleistocene and, at times, may have fallen below its Gibraltar outlet and evaporated to levels below that of the major oceans. In response to their changing base level, the major rivers repeatedly scoured and refilled their channels.

The Present Geologic Status

The Mediterranean region is one of the more complex geological areas on earth and appears as a junction of many plate boundaries and a hodge podge of several ill-defined small plates between the two large plates of Eurasia and Africa. The plate boundaries in the Mediterranean are in need of considerable refinement; however, a general picture will be attempted here (fig. 1).

The writer proposes an active Italian plate, Aegean plate and Turkish plate between the larger Eurasian and African plates. To the east, an Arabian plate is swinging counterclockwise away from Africa and impacting against

Iran; and the Indian subcontinent is attempting to underride the Tibetan Plateau on a dying subduction zone. A double mountain system (fig. 2) from the Alps through the Himalayas suggests the impact of small land masses along much of the south Eurasian margin and their suturing to the Eurasian underside on extinct subduction margins. These sutured land masses are logically represented

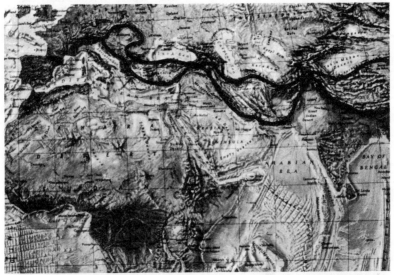

Figure 2. The Double Mountain System on the Southern Edge of the Eurasian Plate.

The northern range begins on the west at the Alps and extends eastward through the Carpathians, Pontus and Elburz to the Kunlun Mountains north of Tibet. In an oversimplified way, these northern ranges have been formed through the impact of island arcs and small continental masses against the underside of Eurasia on subduction zones which are now extinct and have been displaced to the south. These sutured terrains now make up the Pannonian Basin, Anatolian Plateau, Iranian Plateau and Tibetan Plateau.

The southern range begins at the Alps and extends eastward through the Dinarides, Hellenides, Taurus, Zagros and Himalaya ranges and marks the active subduction zones.

by the Pannonian Basin of Yugoslavia, the Anatolian Plateau in Turkey and the Iranian and Tibetan Plateaus to the east. An inland chain of mountain ranges mark the suture zones from the Carpatheans, north of the Pannonian Basin to the Kunlun Mountains north of Tibet, with the Pontus and Elburz Ranges marking the northern edges of the Anatolian and Iranian Plateaus, respectively. The southern margin of these sutured land masses is marked by an active mountain chain beginning in the west, with subduction zone mountains in the Dinarides, Hellenides and Taurus, and ending in the east with the continental impact mountains in the Zagros and Himalayas.

Active divergent plate boundaries, i.e., spreading centers (fig. 3), appear to exist in the Balearic Sea, on the

Figure 3.   Spreading Centers of the Mediterranean.

The Balearic Sea broadens as the Italian plate swings away from Spain, and the Red sea and Aqaba-Jordan rift widens as the Arabian plate swings away from Israel, Sinai and Egypt. The spreading boundary shown north of Greece is a questionable plate boundary with both divergent and shear components.

west edge of the Italian plate; in Northern Greece, on the north edge of the Aegean plate; and in the Red Sea where the rift extends northward through the Gulf of Aqaba to the unique Dead Sea-Jordan Valley.

Strike-slip, transform boundaries (fig. 4) are represented by the Azores-Gibraltar ridge which enters the Mediterranean through the Strait and extends along the North African coast to the Atlas Mountains. The Turkish plate is squeezed westward along the North Anatolian and East Anatolian transform faults to contact the Aegean plate along the West Anatolian fault zone, a boundary of questionable nature.

Figure 4.   Transform Plate Boundaries in the Mediterranean.

The Azores-Gibraltar transform strike-slip boundary enters the Mediterranean at Gibraltar and extends along the African coast to Sicily where it becomes a subduction boundary.

The Anatolian plate is squeezed between Eurasia and Arabia and escapes to the west along very active North and East Anatolian strike-slip faults. The West Anatolian fault zone is a complex plate boundary with convergent and shear characteristics.

Convergent plate boundaries, i.e., subduction zones (fig. 5), are marked by colliding land masses and interior mountain ranges at the Alps, on the north of the Italian plate, and at the Zagros Mountains, on the Arabian-Asian suture. Active subduction trenches exist at the Calabrian trench south of Sicily and the Italian foot, and at the Hellenic trench arcing from the Italian heel south of Greece and Crete, across the southern edge of the Aegean Sea into the Mediterranean south of Turkey to the East Anatolian fault. Cyprus appears to be a wedge of sea floor between branches of the subduction arc. The vulcanism and the

Figure 5.   Convergent Plate Boundaries in the Mediterranean.

Both the Alps and Zagros Mountains are convertent boundaries of continental collision.

The Calabrian arc, south of Sicily, and the Hellenic arc, south of Greece, Crete and Anatolia, are arc-trench systems where ocean crust of the Mediterranean subducts beneath Aegean and Anatolian plates, complete with stratovolcanoes and deep-focus earthquakes a hundred miles, or more, north of the ocean trench.

The eastern edge of Italy overrides ocean crust of the Adriatic Sea as the Italian peninsula closes on the Dalmation coast.

Apennines of the Italian peninsula are best explained by a subduction boundary against the eastern edge of the Italian peninsula in the Adriatic Sea.

Plate motion (fig. 1), described by reference to a fixed Eurasian plate, shows the African plate moving northeast, subducting what little ocean crust remains beneath Greece and Turkey at the Hellenic Arc. The Arabian plate is also moving northeast at an even faster rate, impacting against Iran and rotating counterclockwise away from the African plate along the Red Sea-Jordan Valley rift. The wedge-shaped Turkish plate is moving west on the North and East Anatolian transform faults, as it is squeezed between the Arabian and Eurasian plates and is bumping the Aegean plate which is moving southwest as the overriding plate at the Hellenic Arc. The Italian plate impacting the Eurasian plate at the Alps is swinging counterclockwise over a subduction zone in the Adriatic Sea closing the Adriatic against the Dalmatian coast and enlarging the Balearic Sea to the west.

Geology and the Cultural Development of the Mediterranean

The ancient peoples of western civilization saw the Mediterranean region as the whole of the civilized world and regarded those little known peoples beyond their world as barbarians. Those who inhabited the Mediterranean shores were isolated by geological phenomena. North of the sea were high mountain ranges diverting major rivers away from the Mediterranean and acting as a barrier to migrations and interaction with the peoples of central and northern Europe. South of the sea was a broad impenetrable desert separating the Mediterranean from the cultures of central Africa. The peoples of the Mediterranean formed prosperous seafaring kingdoms, by necessity, and the sea became a broad highway of trade and commerce. Few windows in the self-sufficient, isolated Mediterranean led to the outside world. Beyond the Pillars of Hercules was the vast, open ocean and an occasional contact with the British Isles and the Nordic people. The largest window was at the east end of the sea where the Euphrates and

Tigris Rivers led through the fertile Mesopotamian Valley to the Persian Gulf and the fabled orient. Strong kingdoms in Mesopotamia and the Iranian Plateau repeatedly repelled the armies of the Mediterranean empires, effectively closing the eastern window. Alexander the Great briefly opened the eastern window which also accommodated forays from the east by Mongols, Tartars and Turks.

The Rhone Valley opened into barbaric Gaul; the Nile led to the jungles of east central Africa and cultures of little consequence; and another window opened to the north through the Dardanelles and Bosphorous into the Black Sea and subsequently to the Danube, Don, Dneiper and other river highways of eastern Europe and the steppes of Russia. These highways may have brought Nordic Hittites from Baltic regions and, in post Christian times, they introduced the princes of Russia to the grandeur of Byzantium and the orthodoxy of the eastern church.

Coastlines and harbors are of vital concern to seafaring people and the choice of harbors often foretold the destiny of cities and empires. The southern coasts of the Mediterranean are largely fronted by deserts and drifting sand. Good, protected harbors like those at Carthage were rare indeed, and the coastlines of Libya and Egypt do not have good harbors and are largely uninhabited. Although Alexandria was second only to Rome in the centuries of early Christianity, its harbor is poor and unprotected. Its location on a stabilized off-shore bar on the western tip of the huge fan-type delta of the Nile was wisely chosen by Alexander, since the silt of the Nile distributaries is swept away from the harbor by eastward longshore currents. In recent geologic time, the Nile has introduced sufficient sand and silt into the Mediterranean to build a great delta, of about a 100-mile radius, rounded on the seaward side by the east-moving currents which carry its silt along the coasts of the Sinai and Palestine, producing a straight, sandy coastline. Harbors at Ashdod, Jaffa and Caesarea were man-made with artificial jetties to fend off the advancing sand. Only at Haifa, where Mt. Carmel juts into the sea to defend the Bay of Acre to its north, does Israel have a natural port. North of Haifa the longshore currents have spent their sand, and the highlands on the west edge of the Jordan Valley rift define the coastline. Good harbors begin to appear at Tyre, Beirut and Tripoli.

The entire north coastline of the Mediterranean is mountainous due to active plate subduction or continental collision. The elevated sea level of the world's interglacial sea produces a submergent coastline on these northern shores with a multitude of islands, headlands, embayments and an abundance of large, protected, deep water harbors. Most major empires of classical antiquity developed on the north Mediterranean shores, and cities like Smyrna, Byzantium, Athens, Corinth, Venice, Naples, Genoa and countless others flourished with the trade and commerce of busy ports. Other major cities, limited by a small harbor, and poorly located at the head of a small embayment fed by a minor river, grew to their zenith and then declined as their inadequate harbors silted in. Thus, city giants of the classical era, like Miletus, Ephesus, Troy and others died as their harbors filled with river silt to become malaria-breeding swamps; and today their ruins lie miles from the sea.

Earthquakes occur along all crustal plate boundaries as a result of separating plates, converging plates or plates grinding past one another. The earthquakes of spreading rifts and transform boundaries are shallow focus; however, those caused by plates plunging into the mantle may be shallow or deep and may create epicenters well within the overriding plate. The Red Sea-Jordan Valley rift produced earthquakes of Biblical significance. The plates containing Asia Minor, Greece, Italy and Iran are small and all of these lands are subject to frequent earthquakes. Southern Italy, Crete, Macedonia, West Anatolia, and North Anatolia are especially seismically active and the margin faults of Iran have repeatedly toppled Persian cities. The stone structures of the Greeks, Romans and others were intolerant of shaking ground. As a result, marble temples were repeatedly destroyed and rebuilt, and toppled marble columns are characteristic of most Hellenistic ruins.

Volcanoes have also directed the course of ancient civilizations and are associated with only certain plate boundaries. Spreading boundaries are usually in the seas and are characterized by fissure eruption of fluid basaltic lavas. Occasional basalt flows along the Jordan Valley suggest the spreading environment.

11

Large composite volcanoes, or stratovolcanoes, are confined to subduction boundaries and appear in the Mediterranean north of the Calabrian arc, in Sicily and the Lipari Islands; north of the Hellenic arc, in the southern Aegean Sea and southern Anatolia north of the Taurus Mountains; and along the Italian peninsula, especially in the south. The stratovolcanoes are violent and eject more ash and tephra than molten lava, and may explode and collapse to giant calderas.

Perhaps the greatest explosion the earth has known was the eruption of Thera or Santorini, in the south central Aegean about 1500 B.C. The eruption created a huge submarine caldera of which the modern Santorini islands are a mere shell. It covered much of Crete with deep ash and spread ash across the Mediterranean towards Egypt. The eruption of Thera may have destroyed the Minoan civilization on Crete and stimulated waves of refugees to wash ashore on eastern Mediterranean shores as the mysterious "Peoples of the Sea." Some have even attributed the plagues of Moses to the eruption.

Mt. Vesuvius, on the Bay of Naples, has erupted periodically through historic times since its heralded eruption of A.D. 79. The volcano, known as Mt. Somma, must have been dormant for centuries before it exploded to an open caldera in A.D. 79, burying the Roman city Pompeii with air-fall ash after smothering many of its inhabitants with gasses and dust. Pliny the Elder and many other prominent Romans died in the rain of ash. Only a few miles away Herculanium was overwhelmed by mud flows mobilized by torrential rains, from the electrical storms capping the eruption, falling on slopes of loose ash and dust. Several subsequent eruptions have built a very substantial volcanic peak, Mt. Vesuvius, within the Somma caldera, and have become less violent with shorter dormant periods. Mt. Etna, on Sicily, has erupted frequently through historic time and the mountain and its sulfur mines are often mentioned in ancient history.

The several volcanic islands of the Lipari group, north of Sicily, were anciently known as the Aeolian Islands and were the legendary home of the winds. Mt. Stromboli was the "lighthouse of the Mediterranean" and its neighbor, Mt. Volcano, was the forge of Vulcan and entrance to the underworld.

The stratovolcanoes of central Anatolia are numerous and active. Ash and dust from Mt. Ergeus, Hasan Dagi and other volcanoes filled the valleys of Cappadocia with volcanic ash which subsequently weathered to the cones, pinnacles and "fairy chimneys" of Cappadocia. In these soft ash cones early Christian groups of Cappadocia and Galatia, possibly founded by the Apostle Paul, cut their chapels, homes and hidden underground cities. It was here they sought refuge from the Iconoclastic persecutions and painted their icons on underground walls and ceilings. Here, also, they hid from marauding armies of Arabs, Mongols, Tartars and Turks.

Wherever there were Romans, there were Roman baths; and, wherever there were convergent or divergent plate boundaries, there were hot springs to feed the baths. We know today that thermal waters bubble up along the central axis of the Red Sea rift depositing valuable metals on the sea floor. In ancient times, hot springs along the northward extension of that rift were the sites of elaborate Roman spas like the famous baths at Hammat Pader. Subduction at the Hellenic arc produced not only volcanoes, but abundant hot springs on the Greek islands and the south coast of Turkey; and the west Anatolian fault zone localized thermal springs and white travertine terraces at Hierapolis (modern Pamukkale—"colton fortress") where the ruins of ancient baths cap the terraced mounds and modern tourists swim in the thermal waters just as their Roman ancestors did. Hot springs and calcareous spring deposits are also abundantly associated with the vulcanism of the Calabrian arc and the Italian peninsula. Italian travertine was the "stuff" of many Roman columns, buildings and highways and is shipped throughout the world today.

Other building materials of ancient societies were, likewise, a consequence of their geological settings. The Mesopotamian Valley, the "land between the rivers," was a world of mud and clay. Structures were of mud and clay brick. The finest facades of the king's palace were colorful glazed clay ceramics; and written documents were tablets of clay indented by cuneiform characters.

In Upper Egypt, the Nubian sandstone forms the cliffs flanking the Nile valley, and the monuments of Ramses and the Ptolemaic temples are drab, gray-brown sandstone. The lower Nile cuts Eocene limestones which overlie the Nubian sandstone, and the pyramids are largely soft, tan limestone. In the East Desert, the thermal plateau along the west edge of the Red Sea spreading center has exposed the basement rock of the Arabo-Nubian massif, and there granitic intrusions and metamorphic gneisses were quarried for statues and obelisks. The famous Aswan granite was barged down the Nile to the sea and thence to all parts of the Mediterranean world.

Along the northern Mediterranean coast are the igneous and metamorphic rocks distinctive of subduction zones. The north shore sediments of the old Tethys Sea were largely limestones and their metamorphism yielded marble, the favorite building stone of the Hellenistic period. Marbles were often brecciated by subduction, and the temples, baths, theaters and other public buildings of ancient agoras often contained slabs or columns of brecciated and recrystallized marble. Green serpentine rock, often brecciated, is also common in Greco-Roman structures. It is part of the ophiolite suite which consists of basaltic pillow lavas and peridotites (largely altered to massive serpentine) with accompanying deep-water limestone and chert. Ophiolite rocks are said to represent ocean crust "scraped" onto the overriding plate at subduction trenches.

Metals commonly defined the progressive stages of ancient civilizations. The Copper Age drew heavily from the island of Cyprus, which means "copper," and which is a copper-rich wedge of ocean crust between branches of the Hellenic trench. Egypt mined copper in the central Sinai, and King Solomon's mines in the Wadi Araba supplied copper, bronze and brass for the temple at Jerusalem. Other plate boundaries, both modern and ancient, supplied copper, especially those surrounding Asia Minor which was perhaps the most blessed of all the ancient world with mineral resources. Native copper was used directly; and the ancients quickly learned to reduce the metal from oxides and carbonate ores.

The Bronze Age required the addition of tin which was not common in the Mediterranean region. Minor tin occurred in the Pontus Mountains near the copper deposits at Erzincan in northeast Asia Minor. Mariners brought tin from Spain and ventured beyond into the vast Atlantic to reach the major source at Cornwall, England. Brass, too, was an ancient alloy probably resulting from the accidental smelting of copper ores with naturally associated calamine or smithsonite (i.e.,silicate and carbonate and zinc).

Gold has long been the measure of wealth and has financed the expansion of empires and the luxury of royal courts. It was found as a malleable native metal by patient searchers and molded into offerings to gods and kings. Thermal plateaus on both sides of the Red Sea spreading center expose the granitic intrusions of continental shield rocks, and from this basement complex comes gold. In Egypt, placer gold washed west from the East Desert plateau into the wadis, the Nile and east into the Red Sea wadis. Somewhere east of the Red Sea, wadis also yielded gold in the fabled lands of Ophir and Sheba.

Philip II of Macedonia mined gold from Mt. Pangaion on the spreading plate boundary north of the Aegean plate and, with it, he and his famous son Alexander financed their Macedonian armies which conquered the "world."

Numerous localities in Asia Minor produced gold, and the Greeks told tales of great wealth beyond their domain. King Midas of Phrygia, who ruled from Gordium in central Anatolia and who turned to gold all that he touched, bathed in the Sangarius River which in turn carried gold to Lydia to supply the riches of King Croesus. Lydia was, indeed, the first kingdom to mint gold coins in the sixth century B.C. Jason pursued the golden fleece in the Pontus Mountains of north Anatolia, and other Greek heros returned with riches from Asia Minor.

Silver seemed equally as rare as gold and was largely a product of the mountains and massifs of Asia Minor. Mines near ancient Ephesus supplied silver for the souvenir figures of Diana fashioned by Demetrius and for the silversmiths who threatened the Apostle Paul (Acts 19).

Egypt—the Ideal Land of Antiquity

Each of the ancient civilizations inhabited a site of geographic and geological advantage, but none could surpass the natural advantages of the Nile valley.

(1) Broad, impenetrable deserts flanked the Nile valley to the east and west protecting Egypt from even the most daring invaders. Up river, the Nubian tribes could usually be discouraged by Egypt's awesome reputation symbolized by a colossus of Ramses at Abu Simbel. Down river, the Nile delta exposed a 150 km shoreline to the open Mediterranean, vulnerable to invasion from the sea. Most invading armies, however, followed the natural highway across the northern Sinai so the Egyptian army had to defend a frontier less than 100 km long, between the Mediterranean and the Gulf of Suez, against troops which would have been exhausted by a long desert trek.

(2) The Nile River and its delta distributaries formed the ideal highway system which brought commerce to within a few kilometers of every habitable site in Egypt. The smooth flowing river carried ships and barges northward with its gentle current; and south-bound vessels needed only to raise their sails to catch the northeast trade winds which urged them slowly upstream.

(3) The Nile brought an abundant and dependable supply of water from the tropical rain forests where the rains never failed. While other Middle East and North African nations struggled through periods of drought and famine, Egypt enjoyed blue skies and resourcefully managed its unfailing, unique supply of water. The children of Israel were not the only people to leave a famine-stricken land to seek refuge in the land of the Pharaohs.

(4) Annual floods renewed soil fertility with silt from the African rift and filled countless reservoirs with irrigation water for the coming dry season. For thousands of years, until the building of the Aswan dam, Egyptian farmland remained fertile and during the Roman era was the "breadbasket" of the empire. The flood season also forced peasants from their land onto the desert where Pharaohs organized public-works projects that would ensure their place in history.

(5) The mild climate of the Nile valley and delta was dry, warm and healthful, requiring minimum protection from the atmospheric elements. Rains were rare and winds were seasonal and little more than annoying to inhabitants of the long, narrow empire. Although the Nile valley follows a major fault system which has been somewhat active in historic times, and Miocene volcanic flows were extensive on the western plateaus, Egypt was relatively free of the threat of major earthquakes and volcanoes. Plate boundaries were at least as far away as the Red Sea and the northern Mediterranean and everyday life was secure and easy in Egypt.

(6) The long Nile valley was the only migration highway from the jungles of central Africa to the Mediterranean. Animals from the jungle, huge flocks of water birds and schools of fish moved along the river. Hunting and fishing were good and gave variety and protein to a diet already rich from the produce of an ever-fertile farmland.

The Fayum

In the land of Egypt, which has been repeatedly described as unique, the Fayum valley has its own uniqueness. It is the largest oasis of the west desert (c. 12,000 sq km), a sub-sea level depression separated from the Nile valley by only a few kilometers of desert, partly occupied by a freshwater lake and the only major farmland outside of the Nile valley and delta. Springs discharge clear, pure groundwater, undoubtedly from the influent Nile River, into the depression.

In Paleolithic time the Nile-Fayum divide was breached by a distributary of the Nile and the Fayum depression formed a lake and marshland (Lake Moeris) inhabited by flocks of birds and surrounded by camps of Neolithic hunters. Amenemhat I of the 12th Dynasty (c. 1800 B.C.) took control of the Fayum by constructing earthwork dams at the Nile-Fayum breach. When the Nile was high, he flooded the depression where he held water for the dry season to be released for irrigation on the lower Nile valley and delta. Through the Pharaonic period the

Fayum often languished as swampland between periods of useful water storage.

Greek culture came to Egypt with Alexander in 333 B.C. and thrived under the Ptolemies. About 300 B.C. Ptolemy II (Philadelphus) reclaimed the Fayum valley for agriculture, and Lake Moeris was confined to the present bounds of Birket el-Qarun which lies at the northwest corner of the depression. It measures about 40 km x 10 km and is 45 m below sea level. The Fayum still receives water from the Nile through the Bahr Yusef Canal and is irrigated by a complex network of canals which terminate in the lake. Although the canals drain a highly saline region and the lake lies below sea level with no apparent outlet, the remarkable Birket el-Qarun is only slightly brackish with 1.3% salt content compared to the Mediterranean with more than 3.5% salt.

Ptolemy II constructed cities at several sites in the Fayum, including Karanis, Philadelphia, Bacchias, Philoteris, Dionysias and others, bringing Greek culture and religion there. Julius Caesar, in pursuit of Pompeii, absorbed Egypt into the Roman Empire, and for many centuries the isolated Fayum and its beautiful lake became the vacation retreat and playground of Roman Emperors and their friends.

Christianity came to Egypt very early, and during the second and third centuries Alexandria was a major center of Christian activities and religious study. Controversial Christian leaders and "heretical" Christian sects found a home at Alexandria, and their doctrines flourished in isolated communities throughout Egypt until the Arab conquest. The Fayum communities showed uncommon resistance to Islam and even today retain an unusually large Christian population.

Excavations of the Seila archaeological expedition were begun in February 1981 at Fag el-Gamous on the east edge of the Fayum depression, as a joint venture of the University of California at Berkeley and Brigham Young University. They were continued in February and March 1984 by BYU. They give tantalizing glimpses of a fair-haired Christian community whose doctrines and traditions remain hidden in the sands of the eastern Fayum.

Potential for Geologic 2 and Interdisciplinary Research in and Around the Fayum Depression in Egypt

J. Keith Rigby

Introduction

Even a short visit to the Nile valley and Fayum areas in the Western Desert of Egypt is enough to show the great potential of these areas for research in many disciplines. Let me use geologic research as an example. Much remains to be discovered of the geologic structure and stratigraphy of the area, geologic history, paleontology and details of geomorphic development and their influences on man, from Paleolithic to modern times. The potential for interdisciplinary study is particularly promising in areas where archaeological, geological, botanical, and other scientific research can be integrated. Initial archaeological and geological investigations have been undertaken by the Brigham Young University team in the eastern part of the Fayum depression (fig. 1) near Seila from 1981 through the 1984 field season.

Early in the research project, Revell Phillips and

J. Keith Rigby is professor of geology at Brigham Young University.

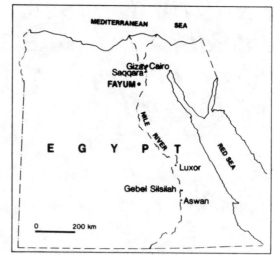

Figure 1. Index map to the Fayum area and possible quarry sites for construction materials along the Nile valley.

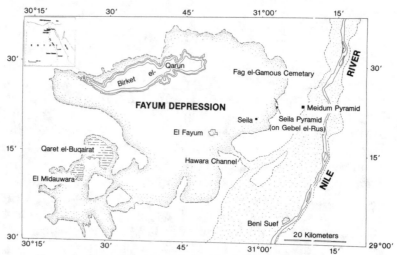

Figure 2. General features of the Fayum Depression and surrounding areas. El Midauwara and Qaret el-Buqairat are salt flats that must have been connected, at times, to the major lake of the Fayum.

Wilfred Griggs became concerned about relationships of bedrock geology and recent deposits to the archaeological sites in the Gebel el-Rus area (fig. 2). Later they additionally questioned uncertainties of origins of the Fayum depression, details of bedrock geology of the Fayum-Nile divide, the chemistry and hydrology of Birket Qarun, the lake that occupies the lowest area of the Fayum depression, and why the lake remains moderately fresh, even though it has been the site of deposition and evaporation for millennia. During the 1980 field season, they also experimented with portable seismic geophysical equipment for location of tombs, etc.

Russell Hamblin undertook a detailed study of bedrock geology in the Gebel el-Rus area around the BYU archaeological site during the 1984 field season as part of the team. It was my good fortune to join the team for a short while and to participate in the multidisciplined investigation of the early cemetery. To Wilfred Griggs of Ancient Studies and Revell Phillips of the Department of Geology at Brigham Young University, I extend my appreciation. It was largely through discussions of their 1981 field activities that we saw the potential for more detailed investigations of the geology and natural history of the eastern Fayum and the area near the Seila Pyramid. It was investigation into materials and sources of material for construction of the Seila Pyramid and popular press notices on construction material of the pyramids at Giza that prompted us to consider further study of sources for materials for other monuments of Egypt.

Sources of Material for Monument Construction

In approximately 400 B.C., Herodotus visited what is now Libya and Egypt and observed the pyramids of limestone, probably in the Giza area. He noted that the limestone contains seashells and concluded that the sea, at one time, covered part of northern Africa because of similarities of the fossil shells to those of organisms then living along the shores of the Mediterranean Sea. He also noted the small fusiform fossils, now known as nummulites, that are common in some blocks, and thought that they were petrified millet that was fed to the workers. He surmised that some millet grains became mixed with the mud and then were turned to stone as the building of the pyramids proceeded. For many years, geologists with greater understanding of limestones have described the pyramid blocks as naturally occurring limestones, probably acquired from the famous quarries nearby.

It appears that we have now gone full cycle. According to the Sunday *Times* (London) of 2 September 1984, Professor Joseph Davidovits, a chemist at Barry University, Florida, has concluded that the slaves in Egypt did not need to haul huge blocks of limestone from the quarries but that the blocks may have been molded at the site of construction of the pyramids at Giza out of cement.

The *Times* noted that from chemical analysis of the pyramid blocks, Davidovits found that limestones from the Turah and Mokattam quarries near Cairo are made of tight calcite crystals, whereas construction stones of the pyramids are considerably less dense and contain many bubbles. He also noted that the limestones of the pyramids contain up to 13% impurities, within the calcium carbonate, such as sodium carbonate, phosphate and silt, which he suggested must have come from the Nile. He also claims to have found other foreign bodies in the stones: organic phosphates like bird droppings, organic fibers like hairs. He concluded that the major blocks comprising the pyramids at Giza probably had different sources from the quarries and that the stones on the outer surfaces of the pyramids were poured like cement to produce a man-made limestone.

The similarity of the blocks that now comprise the major pyramids of the Giza area (fig. 1) to the massive Eocene Mokattam limestones that underlie the pyramids have long since been considered as essentially proven. To those familiar with limestone textures, there is no question about their natural occurrence and origin. The only question is the source quarries. Indeed, there have been few conclusive studies on sources of material for most of the monuments in Egypt. To those, like myself, unfamiliar with details of Egyptian construction and materials, there is a general assumption that sources of construction materials for the major monuments in Egypt have been well-documented and are well-known. It is surprising, even astounding, to find that definitive studies have not been undertaken.

Detailed investigations by Russell Hamblin during the 1984 field season have convincingly demonstrated that the Seila Pyramid on the crest of Gebel el-Rus (fig. 2) was constructed of locally-derived sandstones and limestones. The materials were quarried from Eocene exposures west of the ridge crest. The limestones out of which the pyramids at Giza were constructed have little texture or fabric in common with limestones that were utilized for construction of the Seila Pyramid, although both are roughly the same age. Such differences should allow definition of likely or certain sources.

During the 1984 field season, we visited the Meidum Pyramid, which is approximately nine km east of the Seila Pyramid on the margin of the Nile valley. It would have been an easy, largely downhill, haul to have moved rocks from the Gebel el-Rus down to the Meidum area. However, none of the blocks of the Meidum Pyramid we examined, unfortunately in a somewhat cursory fashion, appear to be locally derived, unlike those of the Seila Pyramid. On the other hand, many look much like chalky limestones of the Eocene Thebes Formation from near Luxor (fig. 1), so well-exposed in major exposures in the vicinity of the Valley of the Kings. These limestones are generally open and porous, smooth and uniformly textured, not like limestones of the pyramids and those found in quarries around Cairo, and not like the limestones of the Seila structure. Similarly, some of the oldest pyramids of the Nile valley at Saqqara (fig. 1) may have been made of blocks that are not of local origin. South of the step pyramid at Saqqara, several moderately deep excavations cut through the bedded limestone and siltstone, suggesting that local building stones may have been available. These rocks appear, again in brief examination, to be different from those used in major construction of temples of the area. These, too, may have been transported downstream, like the granite for statuary at Memphis or the finished granite blocks on the pyramids or Nubia Sandstone in other structures.

Granite and related intrusive igneous rocks used in the Nile valley have been termed the Aswan Granite, but even here, thinking of a single source for the stone near

Aswan (fig. 1) may be somewhat questionable. We need to do a fuller investigation of sources of major construction stones for each of the monuments than has been done in the past. Structures built on both sides of the Nile near Luxor and the major monuments at Karnak include a variety of building stones. Some blocks may have been locally derived from the massive chalky limestone exposed in cliffs above the temples, or they may have been excavated at quarries from the same layers up river. Exposures of similar beds nearby may have been sources for the fine-textured, uniform limestones that were utilized for much of the construction in the middle and lower parts of the Nile valley. For example, limestone for the Meidum Pyramid may have come from quarries up river near Luxor. Currently, we do not know where they come from, and only more research will tell whether these first impressions are even tenable.

On first visits one is so overwhelmed by the awesome architecture of structures at Karnak and the magnificent bas-reliefs that one pays little attention to the basic stones of which the monuments are made. Such was our experience and we need to return to Karnak and each of the major monuments to ask specific questions of origins of materials. We also need to conduct an organized program of evaluation of source materials for individual monuments. It is uncertain, for instance, how much of the material was brought from the Gebel Silsilah area, 65 km north of Aswan (fig. 1), from the granite quarries near Aswan, from possible quarries near Luxor and Cairo, and whether many or few structures were made of locally derived rocks or of transported material quarried from exposures along the margin of the Nile River valley, or elsewhere in Egypt. The various building stones must have distinctive mineralogic and textural "fingerprints" that should allow us to trace their sources and to trace utilization, once their quarries have been identified.

Origin of the Fayum Depression

Various workers (Beadnell, 1905; Sandford and Arkell, 1929; Caton-Thompson and Gardner, 1926, 1929, 1934; Murray, 1951; Pfannenstiel, 1953; Said, 1960, 1962) have speculated both on the origin or origins of the Fayum depression, which now extends to 45 m below sea level, and on the origins of similar depressions across northern Egypt. Origins are still uncertain, however. Most of these topographic low areas appear to lack major bounding faults or folds that would allow easy explanation of the depressions. Some may be depressions cut by streams as sea level was lowered during the Miocene, concurrent with the Messinian dessication of the Mediterranean Sea. For example, the lowering of sea level would have allowed deep erosion of the Nile valley and its tributaries, which are now masked or filled and blocked by subsequent Pliocene deposits. The latter could have filled the channels and connected waterways as sea level rose in the Pliocene. At that time, the Nile valley was flooded, perhaps up to as much as 135 m above present sea level.

Most agents of erosion are limited by sea level, which is essentially the level below which erosion by running water, glaciers, etc., theoretically cannot proceed. Wind in arid environments, however, is one of the agents that may excavate below sea level, as long as the water table is not exposed. Perhaps the Fayum depression owes its origin to deflation in a dry environment when sea level was low.

I suspect that if the origin of the Fayum depression were specifically investigated, we might be able to contribute more than somewhat tangential studies by consistently asking the right questions. Most earlier workers were concerned with regional relationships and had little time to concentrate on possible origins and evidences.

The Fayum basin is rimmed by exposed bedrock, except in one or two possible openings to the Nile valley. To test whether these openings functioned as stream valleys, one would need to test the depth of Pliocene-Pleistocene fillings in them and the depth to Eocene bedrock in the "sill" areas. For example, what is the "sill" depth in the Hawara channel (fig. 2) or in the area of major Pleistocene cover at the southeastern margin of the depression? The Hawara channel and "sill" have reportedly been drilled and the sill is apparently higher than the base of the Fayum basin. However, breccia-based Pliocene deposits may have filled the channel, for it would be possible to confuse isolated Eocene blocks with bedrock. Perhaps geophysical investigations, utilizing the small portable seismic instrument like that used to locate tombs in earlier seasons, might allow confirmation of the sills around the basin. That would eliminate erosion by streams as a possible method of depression development.

Salinity of Birket Qarun

Birket Qarun is a lake 45 m below sea level (fig. 2) and is a remnant of Lake Moeris and probably earlier lakes that occupied the Fayum basin. The depression is a closed basin and appears to have been an area of evaporation. Yet the present lake is not hypersaline but has only approximately half the salinity of the Mediterranean Sea. Such low salinity is unusual, particularly when one considers that gypsum and other saline deposits are common in at least superficial sediments around the lake.

To understand the chemistry of the lake, we need to know how much Nile water has flowed into the depression. We need to investigate the pre-Nile water history of the lake basin and study the sediments for some depth beneath the lake, as well as analyze the chemistry and modern hydrology of the lake. One wonders if some of the saline salts brought into the basin are trapped there. Are there major salt deposits below the clay bottom of the present lake? Are the saline sabkhas of El Midauwara and Qaret el-Buqairat a record of salt withdrawal that helped Lake Moeris remain fresh, like the Gulf of Karabugas helps the Caspian Sea to remain relatively fresh? Is the lake stratified? Is some salt removed from the lake basin by wind action? Are some of the salts along the margin drawn up into plants by wicking, and similarly into porous sediments around the plants by capillary action, only to be blown out of the basin to help maintain moderately low salinity? How could we test the potential of wicking and removal of salt by the wind? Extensive gypsum has cemented aprons of debris in uplands around the Fayum depression. Perhaps these deposits are evidences of salt being removed from Birket Qarun and the Fayum. Is there an asymmetry in development of calcrete around the basin related to prevailing wind or major storm directions? Are the winds really salty and does the wind and wicking produce debris that can be transported out of the basin? We don't know.

Lake Moeris and Birket Qarun Histories

Some early workers (Beadnell, 1905; Caton-Thompson and Gardner, 1929; Sandford and Arkell, 1929; Ball, 1939) wrote short statements about the general physiography of and made preliminary observations on the late Pleistocene-Paleolithic lake and on Egyptian–Roman Lake Moeris (fig. 2). The depression was reportedly converted into a major lake by Amenenhet I and his successors in the 12th dynasty. According to Said (1962, pp.100–01), Lake Moeris was used as a regulator for flow of the Nile, with ponding during flood stages and release of water during low stages; but apparently under Ptolemites, Lake Moeris ceased to be utilized in this way and only the water required for irrigation was then allowed from the Nile valley into the depression. Said (1962, p.101) reported that lacustrine deposits show that the approximate extent of a Paleolithic lake can be traced over a wide area of the depression, rising up to elevations of approximately 40 m above sea level.

Although the preliminary upper boundaries and crude histories may have been established for the lake, essentially, like the upper lake levels of Lake Bonneville were established by G. K. Gilbert, we know little of the vertical fluctuation of the lake, and studies like those done more recently on lake Bonneville need to be done on the Fayum lake or lakes. Investigation of cut terraces and the sediments that accumulated on the terraces and around the basin margin, combined with geomorphic analyses, could document the history of the 80 m of lake fluctuation. Analysis of the sedimentary record in the basin floor could document cycles of rise and fall of the lake. The stratigraphic record of high stands in the eastern part of the basin is preserved in only limited areas and there is some urgency to its investigation.

One wonders about plant succession near the fluctuating shoreline. Where the lake is partially filled in by sediments, the plants certainly will have left a record, if only one of pollen. I suspect that by analysis of cores through sediment fills of Birket Qarun, in the bottom of Lake Moeris, and around its margins, we could see a record of plant utilization throughout the occupation of the depression by man, as well as an earlier Pleistocene plant record. Analysis of cores through sediments may record cycles of Nile flooding and evaporation, as documented by the record of resistant pollen grains.

Analysis of diatoms, small siliceous microscopic plants, from the same cores could also help document changes of environments. I think the record in the bottom of the lake and around its margins will show diatom floral successions and variations as well as utilization of the lake by early Egyptian and Roman flooding and draining. The record might be expected to show the later influence of the Nile River or perhaps the earlier isolation of the basin from the river.

With analysis of the same cores and flanking sediments, we could show rates of addition of salt from the Nile. We should be able to measure introduction of carbonates and sulfates and, certainly, introduction of phosphates by man. With that we should be able to determine rates of sedimentation within the basin itself.

With modest investment in time and equipment, we could do shallow seismic studies across the lake basin using sparker profiling. Such techniques have proven to be effective in generating records in other shallow lakes. Such records may show spring areas within the basin, mark the lateral continuity of layers within the lake basin, and locate possible faults. Such data will tell us much about the history of the basin. We see great potential for interdisciplinary investigation of the Lake Moeris basin and occupation of its margin by paleolithic and later man. Lake cycles have considerable significance to the archaeology and the geologic history of the region.

Geology of the Basin Margin

With the detailed analysis of part of the basin margin by Russell Hamblin, in 1984, we have now looked in detail at far less than 1% of the bedrock of the periphery of the Fayum depression (fig. 2). Similar detailed analyses at selected areas around the basin could tell us much concerning the geology and history of the region. If judiciously located, such key detailed studies could provide correlation points for tying more generalized data into a meaningful network. We know little about the details of the geology of the lake basin. Such studies tied to archaeological studies and related natural and social science studies could produce an unparalleled multidisciplined analysis of a region.

Conclusions

As impressive as our written record will be and as impressive as our research can be in terms of impact on readers, the impact of involvement in a team project on researchers is considerably greater. A continuation and a broadening of the interdisciplinary approach to study of the Fayum area is necessary. For example, chemistry can contribute much about the people and their environment by analysis of trace elements in hair or bones. We need to involve palynologists, botanists, anthropologists, and archaeologists, workers with facility in languages, pathology, dentistry, history, clothing and textiles, zoology, statistics, all of whom could ask questions similar to those posed above and all of whom could help interpret the eastern Fayum.

References

Ball, J. (1939). Contributions to the geography of Egypt. Cairo, Egypt: Survey Dept.

Beadnell, H. J. L. (1905). The topography and geology of the Fayum province of Egypt. Cairo, Egypt: Survey Dept.

Caton-Thompson, G., & Gardner, E. W. (1926). Research in the Fayum. Anc. Egypt, Part I, 1-4.

Caton-Thompson, G., & Gardner, E. W. (1929). Recent work on the problem of Lake Moeris. Geograph. J., 73, 20-60.

Caton-Thompson, G., & Gardner, E. W. (1934). The desert Fayum. London: Royal Anthropological Institute.

Murray, G. W. (1951). The Egyptian climate: An historical outline. Geograph. J., 117 , 422-434.

Pfannenstiel, M. (1953). Das Quartar der Levant II. Die Entstehung der agyptischen Oasendepressionen. Akad. Wissensch. u. Lit. Math. Nat. Kl., Mainz, 7, 337-411.

Said, R. (1960). New light on the origin of the Qattara depression. Bull. Soc. Geograph. Egypteset., 33, 37-44.

Said, R. (1962). The geology of Egypt. Amsterdam-New York: Elsevier.

Sandford, K. S. & Arkell, W. J. (1929). Paleolithic man and the Nile-Fayum divide. Chicago Univ. Oriental Inst. Publ., 1, 1-77.

Paleopathological Observations and Applications At Seila

3

Vincent A. Wood, D.D.S.

*I*n earlier times, those who excavated in archaeological expeditions paid little attention to the human remains they found and often just cast them aside. Around the turn of the century there were few men pioneering in the field of paleopathology (the study of disease in ancient man). Now, there is quite an interest and thousands of individuals in medical and related disciplines are working in this field. Many methods are being utilized and much has been learned. The information found has been of great help to those who study and attempt to reconstruct ancient cultures.

Ways have been found to reconstitute mummified tissue so it can be studied under a microscope. It is also possible to type the blood of mummies. X-rays of pharaonic mummies have verified hieroglyphic genealogies. We don't have space here to go into all the procedures available to study and identify ancient remains; suffice it to

Vincent A. Wood is assistant clinical professor, department of restorative dentistry, School of Dentistry, University of California, San Francisco.

say that methods are extensive and new techniques are continually being developed.

One of the problems in this field in the past is that most of the studies were done in museums or on material that was collected and brought a great distance from the discovery site. This created many problems in identification and non-correlation with the excavation.

For instance, the Royal Ontario Museum in Toronto, studied a mummy in the early 1970's that was encased in a beautiful wooden coffin. The inscription on this case indicated the mummy to be Ta-Khat, a woman from the late 18th dynasty in the court of one of the pharaohs. When the case was opened, the mummy proved to be a male.

Another research team received an elaborate coffin. A dentist in the group, when examining the mummy during autopsy, checked the oral cavity and found a number of very contemporary looking fillings in the teeth. There was also a modern looking mustache on the mummy which ultimately proved to be an English diplomat who had been buried some years before in a British cemetery near Aswan. When Egyptian workers sent the coffin they didn't want to send it empty, so they exhumed this man from a shallow grave and sent him along. These are the kinds of problems that can arise when the study is not done at the site.

There is much to be learned in studying human remains from an archaeological site. Again, at the Royal Ontario Museum in Toronto, a number of leading men in the field of paleopathology performed an autopsy on a male mummy in 1974. He was well identified as a sixteen-year-old weaver from the city of Thebes named Nakht. The autopsy showed a quantity of granite dust in his lungs. As there is no granite in the whole area of Thebes and the closest granite site is 120 miles away in Aswan, the researchers went through some of the legal records found near Nakht's coffin and were enlightened. Apparently, people were punished for minor infractions of the law by being put to work trimming granite from statuary being prepared for pharaonic monuments. From the autopsy, they were able to show that this young man had spent some months in the granite quarries. Paleopathological investigations like this help give a fuller picture than one would perhaps find in any other way.

Not many paleopathology studies have been done on site where medical personnel are able to analyze specimens as they are removed from the ground. That the BYU Seila Expedition is a multi-disciplinary group that can do such studies makes it somewhat unique.

Fag el-Gamous is a large cemetery and a very productive archaeology site. Excavation was done slowly so we could see any artifact that was exposed. Then we worked with a brush and trowel to further uncover what had been found.

When a specimen was unearthed, measurements were recorded to show distance from the sides of the excavation square, and its depth. A catalog number was assigned and photographs taken to show magnetic orientation, size, date and site burial designation (fig. 1). To complete even the

Figure 1.

simplest comparative demographics, several basic determinations were made: for example, determination of sex, age, and measurements taken for the purpose of estimating the living stature. Close observation was also made for any pathological anomalies that might exist. A rather careful examination of the oral cavity and associated structures was made. Notes were taken on the level of dental attrition, missing teeth, extent of periodontal disease, carious lesions, and root surface abrasion.

Several long boards, used as burial sticks, were found in one of the burial sites. (Most of the mummies, when they were well wrapped, had reinforcement poles of various types. Sometimes they were palm fronds that had all of the leaves cut off.) After unwrapping the mummy, we examined the boards closely and discovered rusty nails in them. This seemed unusual for materials so old. We discovered three iron nails, caulking-like material which was jammed into a crack of one board, and a dowel hole which had been plugged. Perhaps these sticks had been parts of some kind of boat; prior to being used as burial sticks.

On most mummies that had wrappings preserved, we found a face bundle. Several layers of material were folded over the face and sewn together. Some face bundles had folded clothing in them. The burial clothes that we found were of many types and colors, many of very fine weave and well preserved. Some of the cloth was so strong we could not tear it. Usually there was a fine outer linen with a stronger wrap inside and a thinner cloth layer below that.

One problem we had in the dig was uncovering human material so rapidly that we had a difficult time cataloging and recording the information. In the first area, we found 23 mummies; in the second area, 24; in another, 30; and in the last one we excavated, there were 47 mummies. Some were well wrapped and others came without preserved burial cloth, in skeleton form. Most of the skeletons couldn't be moved without disarticulating them. We carefully gathered all the pieces, removed them to a protected place and then analyzed them. Some mummies were so well preserved you could see the toe prints.

Now, as we move to a discussion of the dentition, we must mention a rather outstanding specimen that had an excellent set of teeth (fig. 2). It was a female about 23 years of age. She had all her teeth, they were in good alignment, and there were no caries present. She had a normal bite relationship and no periodontal disease. The only problem we could see was a darkness of the enamel layer. In the other mummies we examined, the teeth were not as good.

Figure 2.

Periodontal disease was a major problem in this population. In many mouths, there were calculus or mineral deposits on the labial surface of anterior teeth. This is rarely seen in our modern society because we have toothbrushes. Many teeth were lost from periodontal disease and a few specimens showed osteoporosis in the tooth socket (fig. 3).

As we discussed and analyzed some of the wear characteristics on the teeth of the mummies, we decided to study, for comparison, some of the local Egyptian workers digging at the site. We tried to take pictures of their teeth, but they wouldn't open their mouths and we didn't have

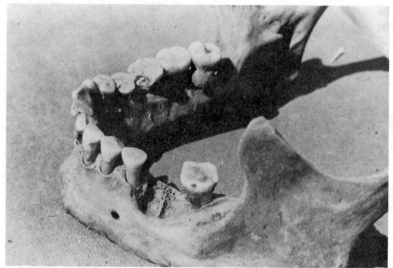

Figure 3.

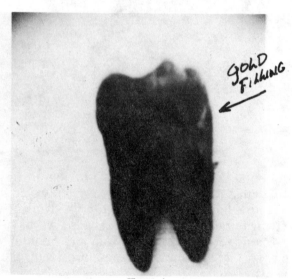

Figure 4.

any retractors. We were able to take only a few pictures of their smiles, but we could see the extensive periodontal disease that is now prevalent in the local community due to lack of oral hygiene. We will discuss the results of the comparisons later in this paper.

Figure 4 is a closeup of a tooth with a gold filling. This tooth was found by our expedition in 1981. Note the gold filling material still in the cavity on the side of the tooth. A gold filling in an upper first molar is impressive and would be difficult to do even today. Whether the decay is out of it or not, we cannot tell. We would like to study this tooth more closely, but unfortunately it has been misplaced in the Cairo Museum. We didn't find any evidence of dental work in the teeth in any of the other mummies. We observed several mummies with a sort of opalescence, (i.e., the enamel doesn't have the normal whiteness). The young lady mentioned in figure 2 had this opalescence. We do not know whether this was a hereditary factor. The mummies with this opalescence nearly all came from the lower part of our excavations where extra moisture might have affected the teeth. We plan to investigate this phenomenon further to try to find a solution.

Anthropologists through the years have written a number of articles concerning tooth attrition in ancient populations. Attrition, wear on the biting surface of the teeth, has been one of the main methods used by researchers to estimate the age of human remains (fig. 5). Categorization of the wear patterns used is fairly complicated. Some investigators contrast the attrition levels between the six- and twelve-year molars, and the wisdom teeth. The eruption dates for these teeth are normally six years apart. Since the purpose of this expedition was not solely to study dental attrition, it was decided that complicated methods of measuring wear were not suitable to the existing situation and a simple four stage comparison was adopted:

"A" = No appreciable wear.
"B" = Wear mostly in enamel; some dentin showing.
"C" = Completely through enamel; well into dentin.
"D" = Wear through dentin; exposed pulp area.

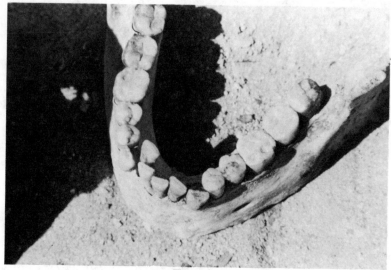

Figure 5.

A general overall-impression of the wear pattern was recorded by the examiner, and each mummy was assigned one of the above stages. We will not include a detailed report of the attrition study findings here, but will only note that a slight majority of the mummies exhibited minor attrition, with 44 of 70 in groupings "A" and "B," and only 10 fit into classification "D," excessive wear.

In many studies of attrition patterns, the common assumption is that wear increases in a more or less direct ratio with age. In our own society there are many variations in occlusal wear patterns and rates not attributable solely to time. Some similar inconsistencies were observed in this study. For example, 11 mummies in the 40–plus age group showed little or no appreciable wear.

Stress and tension are apparently some of the main predisposing factors to bruxism and clenching of the teeth. Individuals with such habits usually exhibit higher tooth attrition than others of the same age. It is likely that ancient man also experienced stress, and this might account for some of the discrepancies observed. Other individual variations that must be considered in analyzing dental wear are the following: heredity, diet, habits, occupation, hardness of enamel and associated structures, malocclusion, pathology, trauma, accidents, loss of teeth and use of teeth as tools.

It has been said that the people in the rural areas of Egypt today live much as they did in ancient times. With this thought in mind, we undertook a study of the dentition of 16 local workers employed as diggers at the site. They all lived within 1 or 2 km of the cemetery site and their average age was 32 years. (This matched closely the average age of the mummies in this study.) Lack of dental care was apparent, with generally poor oral hygiene, and observation of modern attrition patterns produced unexpected results:

Category	1984	Ancients
A (little or no wear)	50%	24%
B (some wear in dentin)	44%	44%
C (wear well into dentin)	6%	2%
D (wear into pulp)	0	15%

F. F. Leek, a British peleopathologist, reports that ancient people introduced small quantities of brick dust, chalk or fine sand in the process of milling their grain. Obviously these materials in bread would cause an increase in the rate of attrition. Today, the Egyptian government provides bread milled by modern methods.

Because many conditions may influence attrition of the teeth, we conclude that dental attrition remains a relatively unreliable method of aging human remains.

In a modern dental practice, the dentist sees many patients exhibiting abrasion on the root surfaces of their teeth. This is generally referred to as cervical abrasion. There is not complete agreement as to which etiological factors are responsible for this destruction of the tooth surface. Two main theories have been proposed by researchers in the field to explain inconsistent patterns of abrasion. The most predominant theory identifies energetic toothbrushing as the principle factor. There is an increasing group of

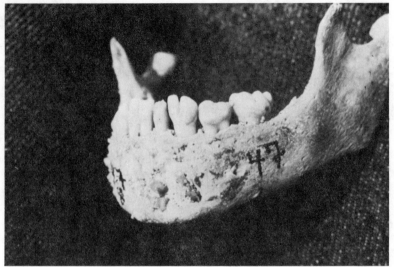

Figure 6.

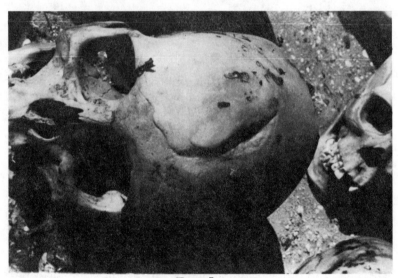

Figure 7.

adherents, however, for the theory that cervical abrasion is caused by flexing and torsional forces on the tooth as it bends slightly from the stresses of bruxism and heavy chewing. When we had almost completed our excavations and were contemplating the demographic implications, we realized that, in all of our observations, we had not noticed any examples of root surface abrasion. This observation certainly is noteworthy. After returning from Egypt, we noted reports of other excavated collections that also record little to no abrasion on the root surfaces of large numbers of individuals. The implications of this phenomenon which is predominant in modern societies and rare in ancient peoples are surely challenging. It is tempting to present one's considered explanations to lend support to whichever theory one espouses, but at this time we do not have sufficient data to draw valid conclusions. I cannot resist noting, however, that both theories lose some credibility as we observe mummies exhibiting extensive attrition (even into the pulp chamber) while showing no cervical destruction.

As we studied the mummies, we noted other anomalies. Two teeth of one child had formed together (fig. 6). This is referred to as concrescence. One skull had a suture line across the middle of the frontal bone. This occurs in 1 to 2% of the modern population and it is called metopism, or a metopic suture. We observed several instances of wormian suture lines. These are highly irregular and meandering sutures in the occiput region of the skull. Several skulls we exhumed, showed evidence of traumatic injury. One chap had three clearly delineated slices into the skull which made us think he might have been struck by a sword or axe. Because the edges of these lesions were still sharp, we might conclude that these blows, or others received elsewhere, were fatal. In macabre contrast, another skull exhibited a large wound that had completely healed with bone filling in the defect (fig. 7). The blow was struck in the middle of the frontal bone or forehead and fractured the skull for a distance of 5 to 6 centimeters, even displacing the nasal bones. We can but conjecture on

Figure 8.

the life he lived or the pain he endured, but we do know that he lived long enough for the bone to heal.

After we finished our examinations, we reburied the skulls so that we will be able to retrieve them next year. We are looking forward to this as there are several interesting things we want to check. The defect shown in figure 8 is one of them. As we reviewed the films we noticed this very unusual lesion on the mandible about 3 cm in diameter. I have shown the pictures of it to several well-known pathologists at the University of California, San Francisco, and none of them has been able to say with certainty what might have caused the defect. It doesn't seem to be invasive into the bone and the way the edges are a bit rolled and rounded suggests it was starting to heal. The overall appearance suggests pressure as one might observe in a

Figure 9.

cyst or some other soft tissue lesion. One pathologist suggested that perhaps a glancing blow from a sword that almost missed could have sliced off a thin layer, and then the wound started to heal. Next year we would like to examine this skull closely with X-rays and other tests.

Many exhumed bones had clear, colorless, slightly opaque crystals extruding from the surface of the lamina dura. The crystals were quite varied in size and shape. We observed some that twisted into a regular spiral, others formed stubby traditional crystalline prisms, and there were a few that were as thin as thread, 2–3 inches long (fig. 9).

After we had finished analyzing and cataloging the mummies, we reburied them in one of the larger pit tombs. The skulls were carefully placed in a shallow pit and gently covered with desert sand for protection until next year.

Now that we have a building to store specimens for further work and extensive study we will not have to resort to reburial.

We hope that in this limited presentation you have been able to see some of the potentialities that are just over the horizon in this field. There are many possibilities for exciting discoveries in the future with numerous questions remaining to be answered. It all is quite fascinating and extremely rewarding.

The Geology of the Gebel El-Rus Area and Archaeology Sites in the Eastern Fayum, Egypt

4

Russell D. Hamblin

*T*he Gebel el-Rus area is part of a 40 square mile archaeological site in the eastern Fayum in Egypt that Brigham Young University has received permission from the Egyptian government to study and excavate. Faculty members in the departments of Ancient Studies and Geology at Brigham Young University decided that analysis of the geology of the excavation sites and surrounding areas would be of geologic interest and would support the archaeological investigation. This paper will provide detailed stratigraphic and lithologic information on the area. Plans for additional archaeological and geological investigations on this historic area are also under consideration.

Some of the best exposures of Tertiary rocks in the

Russell D. Hamblin is a master's graduate in geology from Brigham Young University.

West Desert of Egypt are found on Gebel el-Rus, along the divide between the Nile valley and the eastern Fayum. The western face of this divide is a relatively steep escarpment that rises from 20 m above sea level to the peak north of the Seila Pyramid at about 100 m. Barren Eocene and Pliocene strata are exposed on the ridge and over-look the lush cultivated fields of the Fayum depression.

Rocks are well hidden under a thick alluvial cover on subtle slopes on the eastern side of Gebel el-Rus and along the entire east face of the Nile-Fayum divide. The green Nile River valley and steep-walled Meidum Pyramid, 10 km east of Gebel el-Rus, are on lower slopes and valley fill.

Gebel el-Rus, a rather small mountain covering only about 8 sq. km, contains many interesting geologic features. An angular unconformity between Eocene and Pliocene beds, Pliocene paleochannels filled with debris-flow deposits, a variety of sedimentary structures, trace fossils, and distinctive faunas are some of the important aspects of the area that require local detailed studies.

There has been a lack of even moderately detailed geological studies in the eastern Fayum with respect to stratigraphy, paleoecology, and sedimentary petrology of the Eocene rocks.

Environments of deposition of rocks exposed in escarpments and hills around the Fayum depression and in surrounding regions have been discussed in a regional way by early workers, including studies by Beadnell (1905), Sanford and Arkell (1929), and Shata (1975). However, these and other studies have differed in interpretation of the stratigraphic section and its history. This study concerns a relatively small area with good exposures that was examined intensively in order to document evidences of environments and geologic history of these Tertiary rocks and to compare these data with those obtained by earlier regional studies.

Geological methods applied in this study to document rocks, structures, and faunas include the following: measurement and description of eight stratigraphic sections, correlation of the various lithologic units and subunits between sections, construction of a geologic map on a scale of approximately 1:13,000, lithologic descriptions, and evaluation of paleontologic data.

This study involves strata exposed on the western face and crest of Gebel el-Rus, which forms part of the escarpment ridge at the eastern edge of the Fayum depression. Gebel el-Rus is on the Nile valley-Fayum depression divide, approximately 8 km northwest of Seila, Egypt. The area is centered at approximately 29 degrees 24' north latitude and 31 degrees 3' east longitude (fig. 1 & 2).

The earliest geological studies of the Fayum were conducted in the 1890's by M. Blackenhorn (1901, 1902), in which he discussed many of the geomorphological features of the depression and surrounding areas. Hugh J. L. Beadnell (1901, 1905) published some of the most extensive work ever done on the stratigraphy and lithology of Lower Eocene through Recent strata of the Fayum. Subsequent papers by Elinor W. Gardiner (1927, 1929, and 1934), K. S. Sanford (1929), O. H. Little (1936), R. Said (1962), and Tamer (1975) are largely follow-up studies of Beadnell's earlier observations. Most of these publications emphasize the regional geology of the Fayum depression, but many local areas were studied with little detail.

Studying in a foreign land can often be difficult and challenging because of differences in laws, language, and culture. Several Egyptians provided essential help to the archaeology project and to this geological study. I express my appreciation to the following: Dr. Ahmed Kadry, director of the Egyptian Antiquities Organization, Ali Khouly, director of Antiquities for Middle Egypt and former director of Antiquities for Middle and Lower Egypt, and members of the Permanent Committee of the Egyptian Antiquities Organization for granting Brigham Young University permission to excavate and work at the site of Seila. Appreciation is also expressed to the following for giving support and assistance to the research team during the 1984 season: Mr. Moustafa el-Zairy, chief inspector at Beni Suif, Mr. Ali Bazidi, chief inspector at Fayum, Mrs. Sami, inspector at Fayum, Mr. Akram Eshak, inspector at Fayum and inspector working with the excavation team on the site, and Mr. Sabri Gabbour, director of the museum at Kom Aushim. I also wish to thank Ramaddan Absed Mohammed and Abdel Setar Ahmed, who assisted and

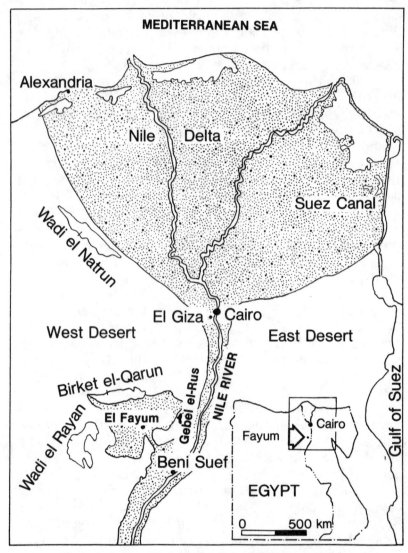

Figure 1. Index map of Egypt and the Gebel el-Rus area.

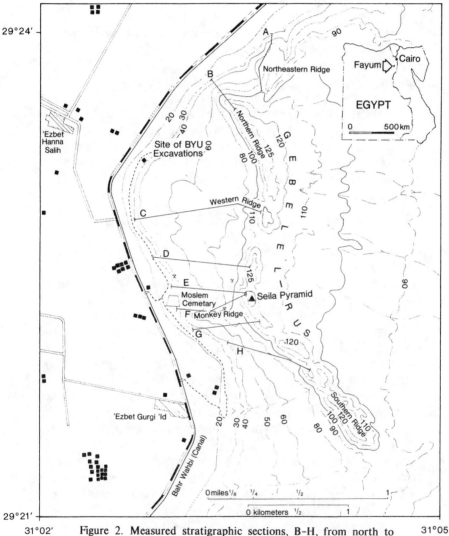

Figure 2. Measured stratigraphic sections, B–H, from north to south along Gebel el-Rus.

accompanied me in the field during my geological excursions at the site. Partial support for the study was provided by the Mormon Archaeology and Research Foundation, and Mr. Wallace Tanner, its president and founder.

Dr. J. Keith Rigby, chairman of the thesis advisory committee, and Drs. Jess R. Bushman and Wm. Revell Phillips, were members of the committee. Thanks is also given to Dr. C. Wilfred Griggs, director of Ancient Studies at Brigham Young University and the director of the project in Egypt. Dr. Phillips invited me to participate with the group. Phillips Petroleum Company and Marathon International Oil Company provided financial support for field work and thesis preparation. Staff personnel at Phillips Petroleum Company prepared many of the necessary thin sections of rocks and fossils from the study area. Micro-faunal identification and interpretations were provided by Dr. Stanley H. Frost.

Regional Structural Relationships

Said (1961), in describing the tectonic framework of Egypt, concluded that the country is composed of three structural units: the Arabo-Nubian massif, the stable shelf, and the unstable shelf. The Arabo-Nubian massif is the basement core, and these rocks are well exposed east of the Fayum in major ranges of the southern Sinai and along the Red Sea in the East Desert of Egypt.

The Arabo-Nubian massif is overlapped and surrounded by the stable shelf, an area of thin continental and epicontinental Cretaceous and Cenozoic units. The Upper Cretaceous-Lower Tertiary shallow-water Nubian Sandstone is overlaid by Eocene rocks, part of which were investigated in this study. The Eocene shale, limestone, and sandstone represent a major marine transgression that covered the stable shelf. The transgression of the sea began near the Late Cretaceous-Early Tertiary transition and ended with a regression that took place from the Middle Eocene to near the close of the Oligocene.

The stable shelf, according to Said (1961, p. 200) is characterized by the thinness of the sedimentary section, minor normal faulting, and the basin producing rift zones of the Red Sea–Suez region. Although major anticlinal features are lacking in the stable shelf, there are several domes that have broad and gentle flanks on all sides. Minor movement of these structures has produced local diastems rather than major unconformities.

Most of northern Egypt is considered part of the unstable shelf or mobile belt (Henson, 1961: 199). Compressional stresses responsible for SW-NE, NW-SE, and E-W trending folds and faults mainly began in Middle and Late Cretaceous time. Because of the incompetent nature of rocks of the unstable shelf, internal stresses were relieved through tensional movements and normal faulting resulted when compressive stresses were released.

The Fayum area lies within Said's stable shelf. Areas west of Gebel el-Rus and the Nile-Fayum divide, in the West Desert of Egypt, have been extensively faulted and folded. To the east, the Nile valley is also fault controlled. The Fayum depression and its surrounding escarpments, however, have escaped the effects of major faulting and folding. Gebel el-Rus area lacks any significant faults, but minor tilting of Eocene strata is apparent. A gentle northward dip of 3 degrees to 8 degrees of Middle and Upper Eocene rocks produced a subtle but observable angular unconformity between these rocks and overlying, essentially horizontal, Pliocene deposits.

According to Tamer (1975: 21), the Fayum depression overlies the axis of a major anticline and is affected by normal faulting. He described a great monoclinal edge that bounds the depression on the northern and eastern sides.

Eocene Deposits

Eocene strata exposed on the western flanks of Gebel el-Rus are represented by Middle Eocene Ravine beds and Upper Eocene Birket Qarun Formation. The Birket Qarun Formation was named from the large lake, Birket el-Qarun, which occupies the northern edge of the Fayum depression. The Ravine beds conformably overlie the Wadi el-Rayan Formation to the south and southwest of the Fayum depression. Middle Eocene Wadi el-Rayan rocks are composed of interbedded nummulitic limestones, reefal limestones, and shaly sandstones according to Beadnell (1905: 35-37). A marly limestone containing *Nummulites gizehensis*, a rather large foraminifera, marks the top of Wadi el-Rayan strata and base of the overlying Ravine beds. The Wadi el-Rayan Formation, although of different lithology, correlates, in time, with the lower Makattam Limestone exposed in major quarries near Cairo. Lithologic and paleontologic evidence suggests shallow water and warm climate during deposition of the Wadi el-Rayan and Ravine sediments.

The Birket Qarun Formation, which overlies the Ravine beds on Gebel el-Rus and northward, is overlain by the Qasr el-Sagha formation north of the Fayum depression. Qasr el-Sagha units are correlative to the upper Makattam or Maddi Formations near Cairo. Best exposures of these deposits are on steep escarpments immediately north of Birket el-Qarun. Qasr el-Sagha strata are characterized by argillaceous sandstones, mudstones, and limestones. Many important terrestrial vertebrates and *Carolia placunoides*, *Ostrea fraai*, and other marine fossils are present in these Bartonian age rocks.

The faunal association found in the Qasr el-Sagha Formation indicates accumulation in nearshore, shallow seas with adjacent fluvial systems. Such a relationship would be required for terrestrial vertebrates to be deposited together with marine mollusks.

The overlying estuarine Oligocene Qatrani Formation and nearshore deposits from the Qasr el-Sagha Formation are evidences of marine regression or shoreline progradation. According to Issawi (1972) several other sedimentary sequences deposited in northern Egypt indicate that the Tethys Sea regressed to the north during late Eocene and Oligocene times.

Stratigraphic Nomenclature

Beadnell's stratigraphic nomenclature (1901 and 1905) included Lower Eocene beds in the Wadi el-Rayan series, Middle Eocene beds in the Ravine beds, and Upper Eocene in the Birket Qarun series and Qasr el-Sagha series. Said (1962: 101), however, used more formal stratigraphic nomenclature for the same units: Lower Eocene Wadi el-

Rayan Formation, Middle Eocene Ravine beds, and Upper Eocene Birket Qarun Formation, and Qasr el-Sagha Formation. The present study emphasizes details of the Ravine beds and the overlying Birket Qarun Formation of the Eocene series.

According to Beadnell (1905: 42), some 60 m of strata forms the major section of the cliff that rises above the northern shore of the lake Birket el-Qarun. The basal 15 m of the Birket Qarun Formation is preserved on the northern flanks of Gebel el-Rus, in the research area. However, northwest of the Fayum depression, on Gebel Gehannam, the Birket Qarun Formation is over 50 m thick, and underlies the Qasr el-Sagha Formation. Middle Eocene strata exposed on Gebel Gehannam, referred to as the Gehannam Formation by Said (1962: 101), are correlative to the Ravine beds exposed on Gebel el-Rus.

Beadnell (1901: 37) named the exposed strata, bordering the arable fields of the Fayum oasis on the west, north, and east sides, the Ravine beds. This series is also exposed in el-Butts and el-Wadi ravines, both of which cut across the cultivated fields of the depression. Consistent ravine exposures of these Middle Eocene deposits explains the unit name.

Several resistant Middle and Upper Eocene ledge-forming subunits are well exposed in the study area. Many of these are well-lithified calcareous sandstone and sandy limestone beds that are interbedded with shaly slope-forming marly beds. These key units are easily differentiated and correlated on the western flanks of Gebel el-Rus and have been given the following informal field names by the writer; from the bottom up, the "graveyard limestone," "quarry limestone," "orange limestone," and "contact sandstone." Each of these units is discussed in the description of Eocene deposits (fig. 3).

Lithologic Description

Eocene strata exposed in the Gebel el-Rus area are characterized by a variety of calcareous-clastic sediments that range from slightly calcareous mudstones to calcareous sandstones or sandy packstones. Rocks with small amounts of calcium carbonate composed 60 to 70 percent

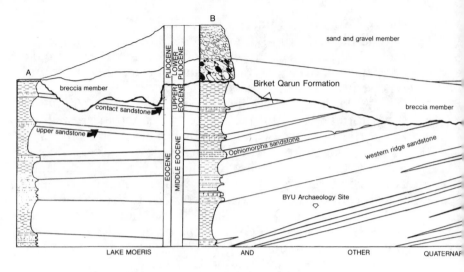

Figure 3. Measured stratigraphic Sections A–H with correlation of various units exposed in the study area.

of the entire Eocene section and the remaining 30 to 40 percent are rocks with moderate to large amounts of calcium carbonate.

Topographic expression of Middle and Upper Eocene units is largely controlled by the amount of calcium carbonate present in the rocks. Lithologic units with little calcium carbonate cement form slopes and recesses; they remain poorly lithified and are easily eroded. Calcareous units, however, are well lithified and form minor cliffs where they are thick bedded, or resistant ledges where thin bedded. Gypsum, as lenses or veins, may also be responsible for steep cliff-like slopes. Gypsum commonly fills fractures as veins in massive rocks and as concave-up, lense-like structures in thin cross-bed sets. Gypsum is usually not very resistant to erosion, but, in the desert, it forms weakly resistant ledges and ridges.

The most abundant rock types of the Eocene section in the study area are mudstones and argillaceous siltstones. These fine-grained clastic deposits form wide, gentle slopes and broad, flat areas where the deposits are thick and they erode to recessive units or undercuts that separate more

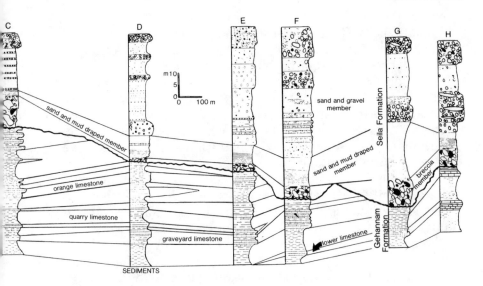

Figure 4a. Generalized stratigraphic section of Tertiary units exposed in the Gebel el-Rus area.

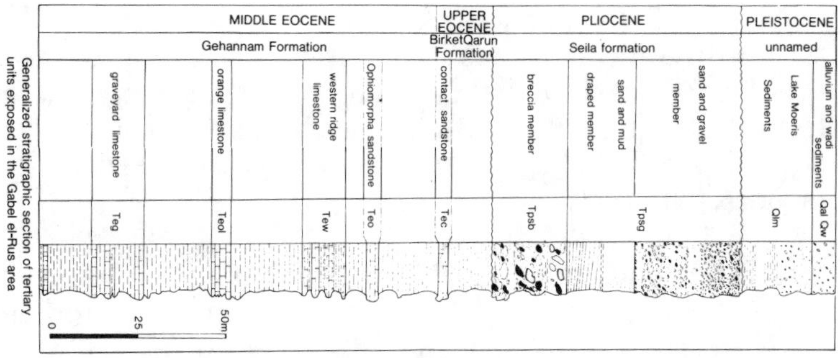

Figure 4b. Generalized block diagram of the eastern Fayum region (Gebel el-Rus area) during Eocene to Oligocene-Miocene times. Eocene units were exposed, uplifted, and gently folded. Volcanism was also associated with upwarping. Study area marked with an arrow.

resistant beds. These deposits, poor in calcium carbonate, are generally brownish and olive gray under a veneer of loose debris or gypsum-cemented lag.

Eocene strata made up of units with moderate to large amounts of calcium carbonate are marls, silty marls, calcareous sandstones, and sandy limestones or packstones. These units form steep slopes, when moderate calcium carbonate is present, and ledges and minor cliffs, when the units are rich in calcium carbonate.

Limestones that lack abundant terrigenous material are generally thick bedded and massive. Where terrigenous clastic materials increase so do trace fossils and sedimentary structures, such as bidirectional short-wavelength ripple marks, cross-laminations that generally trend N125E, and load casts from 10 cm to 1 m in diameter. Calcareous sediments range from yellowish-orange to grayish-orange. Rocks that lack abundant clastic constituents, such as chalky and pure limestones, tend to be very pale orange to very light gray or nearly white.

Well lithified, thick-bedded limestones, packstones, and wackestones in the study area have been used as building stones for centuries, as evidenced by several building structures and many worked quarries. Building stones for the third Dynasty Seila Pyramid were apparently quarried from these sites. Recent tool markings and dynamite scars are evidences that these quarries have also been used for modern buildings.

Petrographic analysis shows that these rocks are texturally and mineralogically submature. Grain size ranges from coarse silt to fine and medium sand, and grain framework from sorted to fairly well sorted; the sand grains are mostly angular and subangular. Only a few grains have rounded edges or corners, but most approach equant shapes.

All terrigenous units are dominated by quartz although the framework of many contain an array of accessory minerals, e.g. plagioclase, microcline, hornblende, biotite, muscovite, zircon, polycrystalline quartz, and quartz with minor fluid inclusions. Angular calcite fragments and rounded glauconite grains are present in many samples.

The presence of these accessory minerals indicates a granitic source. Clays rich in hematite and limonite form the matrix in most units and cements are usually microsparite and micrite.

Subdivision of Eocene Strata Based on Resistant Units

Middle and Upper Eocene deposits exposed on the western flanks of Gebel el-Rus were subdivided on the basis of alternating major resistant ledge-forming and slope-forming units. Thick resistant limestone units range from 1 to 3 m thick and are generally packstones and wackestones. Minor subunits form ledges 0.5 to 1.0 m thick and usually consist of sandy marl and silty limestone. Some key units may contain two to four ledges. Ledges are separated by thin, recessive beds, usually mudstones.

Informal subdivisions of the Middle Eocene exposed in the study area are, from bottom to top: "graveyard limestone", "quarry limestone", "orange limestone", "western ridge sandstone", "*Ophiomorpha* sandstone", "last sandstone", and "contact sandstone". These resistant units are easily correlated between measured sections and are separated by units of mudstone or argillaceous siltstone that form broad slopes or covered intervals (fig. 2).

Facies Interpretations

Most of Egypt was covered by a warm, shallow sea during the Early and Middle Eocene that resulted from a major marine transgression of the Tethys Sea. Marine sediments were deposited on deformed Cretaceous rocks in northern Egypt. Thick Paleocene and Eocene sections accumulated in structural basins but Eocene deposits are thin and Paleocene deposits are missing over anticlinal highs. According to Salem (1976: 34), well data reveals such basins separated by elongated structural ridges.

Deposition of fluvial and interdeltaic facies north of the Fayum depression are the result of shoreward progradation coupled with a northward regression of the sea during the Late Eocene and Early Oligocene. The Fayum region was later an area of topographic prominence due to crustal upwarping during the Oligocene and Miocene. Thus, the study area was subaerially exposed beginning in the Oligocene and remained so until it was invaded by an arm of the Mediterranean Sea during the Pliocene.

Deposits of the Middle Eocene Ravine beds and Upper Eocene Birket Qarun Formation exposed in the study area accumulated in transgressive and regressive shallow seas. Sandy carbonate units interbedded with mudstones represent oscillations between high and low energy states. Ledge-forming calcareous sandstone beds, such as the "*Ophiomorpha*" and "contact" sandstones were deposited in higher flow regimes than the silty mudstones that occur below and above each unit. Finer sediments were winnowed away in the strong currents that deposited the sands. Firm substratum, of thick sand accumulation, provided suitable environments for such organisms as clams and oysters.

Faunal assemblages from Ravine bed and Birket Qarun strata in the study area are good indicators of subtropical, shallow seas at the Late Eocene-Middle Eocene interphase. Nummulitid foraminifera, sessile benthonic organisms in sublittoral neritic zones, are often abundant in many exposed sandy carbonate beds. Modern large foraminifera similar to ancient nummulites live in shallow seas of the tropics.

The "orange limestone" contains frequent clusters of nummulites that were either used by other organisms to fill or to line shallow burrows, or they crawled into the burrows themselves to escape dessication in very shallow water. This and many other units contain scattered microscopic echinoid spines and plates, oyster and clam shell fragments, and bioturbated beds. Although some sedimentary structures are present in many sandy carbonate beds on Gebel el-Rus, most bedding is massive, the stuctures having been largely destroyed by bioturbation, possibly by the burrowing of sediment-feeding clams. These findings indicate that abundant life processes and moderate to strong currents were factors of the environment during deposition.

Many of the preserved sedimentary structures give evidence of nearshore shallow seas. Short wavelength, cross-lamination structures are present in a few of the ledge-forming units. The "*Ophiomorpha* sandstone" contains the best example of cross-bedding. Well preserved ripple-drift, cross-laminated sets in this unit indicate rapid subaqueous deposition by currents with moderate flow regimes. The bidirectional pattern of the cross-laminations in many sandstone units is evidence that tidal currents were important factors of the environment during sedimentation. Hummocky cross-bedding in the "contact sandstone" presents the possibility that many of these calcareous sands were deposited during storms or other violent events.

Undulating contacts between shaly units and overlying sandstones and loadcast structures into mudstones are abundant in the higher subunits of the study area. The "western ridge sandstone" and "*Ophiomorpha* sandstone" contain such structures, although the best examples are the "contact sandstone" where large, bulbous loadcast structures, nearly a meter in diameter, protrude down into the underlying mudstone bed. Contact irregularities and loadcasts result either from calcareous sands rapidly deposited on the muddy floor of a regressive sea or from storm-driven sand deposited over mud in a transgressive sea.

Moderate amounts of plagioclase, microcline, hornblende, and other chemically unstable minerals indicate that the sandy carbonate sediments are mineralogically submature. Although grains are generally sorted, they range from angular to subrounded and these sediments are also considered texturally submature. The presence of feldspars, micas, hornblende, and other unstable accessory minerals in these Eocene rocks indicate a granitic source terrain not far from the site of deposition and minimal reworking of the sands after deposition.

Pliocene Deposits

Most high level ledges and cliffs on Gebel el-Rus are horizontal Pliocene deposits. Ridge-forming breccia deposits, composed of large subangular blocks detached from numerous Eocene units, are the earliest Pliocene deposits in the section. Laminated sands and sandstones which drape over these beds form steep slopes and are overlain, in turn, by ledge- and cliff-forming gravelly sandstones and sandy conglomerates.

Aigner (1983) described Pliocene deposits near Cairo, on the Giza Pyramids Plateau, which are similar to the breccia deposits on Gebel el-Rus. According to Aigner (1983: 319), large blocks from Eocene bedrock were detached by erosive wave action accompanying a transgressing Pliocene gulf.

According to Said (1981), the Pliocene gulf flooded the Nile River valley from the Delta to Aswan. In this estuary, 12 km wide and over 1300 km long, over 460 m of sandstone and sandy mudstone and over 1500 m of shale were deposited at the Abu Madi Formation and Kafr el-Sheikh Formation respectively. Several other Pliocene gulf deposits are discussed by Said (1981: 100-101).

Stratigraphic Nomenclature

The Pliocene deposits of Gebel el-Rus are here subdivided into three distinct beds—coarse breccia blocks, laminated sandstone drape, and sandy, gravelly conglomerates, or lower member, middle member, and upper member.

No formal lithostratigraphic names have been applied to Pliocene deposits of the Fayum region. Lithologies and deposition environments were used by early workers to describe the Pliocene rocks. For example, Beadnell (1905: 37) noted strata exposed high on Gebel el-Rus and called them Pliocene gravel terraces; Said (1962: 105) called the same deposits Pliocene estuarine and fluvitile gravels; and Little (1963: 228) described the coarse breccia deposits in the Fayum region and called them Pliocene slipped masses.

Pliocene deposits in the Gebel el-Rus were, in this study, subdivided lithologically for an informal nomenclature. The oldest and lower member of the Pliocene is here termed "breccia beds." This unit, at the Eocene-Pliocene contact, is composed of large reworked subangular blocks of Eocene units. Two types of breccia have been recognized in this study: channeled debris flow deposits and nonchanneled, or sheetlike, debris flow deposits.

The middle Pliocene member is a unit here termed "Pliocene sand drape." These laminated sands and sandstones overlie the "breccia beds" with a sedimentary dip. The "Pliocene sand drape" member is named from the unusual manner in which the clean, poorly lithified sands and sandstones drape over the irregular debris flow deposits.

The upper member of the Pliocene is here termed the "sandy, gravel conglomerate" member. Poorly sorted and lithified sandy gravels, gravelly sandstones, and gravelly conglomerates form the prominent ledges, cliffs and peaks on Gebel el-Rus.

Lithologic Description

Relatively dark Pliocene deposits overlie and cut into light-toned Eocene rocks with angular discordance. Pliocene deposits range from the lower coarse subangular debris flows to middle laminated interbedded sand, unlithified clay; and sandstones to gravelly sandstones and sandy, gravelly conglomerates of the upper units. These Neogene rocks form prominent cliffs and ledges on the western face of the north-south ridge of Gebel el-Rus but blanket the gentle eastern slope that sweeps down to the Nile valley. The highest altitude of Pliocene sediment in the study area is the cap on "northern ridge" and its lowest outcrop is only 30 m above sea level on the east-west "monkey ridge."

The oldest Pliocene deposits on Gebel el-Rus, here termed the "breccia bed" member, are composed of subangular blocks of Middle and Upper Eocene calcareous sandstone. These blocks range from 0.5 to 3.0 m in diameter and occur in lenses and irregular sheets that overlie and partially truncate Middle and Upper Eocene strata. Many of these grayish-orange, Eocene-derived blocks are fossiliferous, containing shelled invertebrate faunas such as Middle and Upper Eocene nummulites, turritellid gastropods, and bivalves (clams and oysters). Some blocks are essentially oyster coquinas and other less fossiliferous blocks contain a few *Ophiomorpha* and *Thalassinoides* trace fossils and faintly preserved, small-scale ripple marks and cross-laminations. Some of the nonfossiliferous sandy limestone blocks are concretionary. Blocks of the "breccia beds" member are densely packed and surrounded either by a poorly lithified sandy-silty matrix or a partially lithified, argillaceous matrix.

"Breccia beds" that are lenticular are here termed "channeled debris flow deposits" and form prominent ridges on Gebel el-Rus (i.e. "northern ridge," "western ridge," and "monkey ridge"). These deposits range from 10 to 30 m deep, from a few meters to over 120 m wide, and from 10 m to nearly 1 km long.

Sheet-like breccia deposits are continuous with the debris-filled lenses and conjoin the ridges as nonchanneled debris flows. These sheet-like accumulations have a poorly lithified matrix of fine-grained sand and silt without significant mud or clay. Channel fill and sheet-like breccia deposits are apparently contemporaneous.

Breccia deposits in the study area, excluding those on "northern ridge," are overlain by poorly lithified sandstones that appear to grade continuously upward from the sandy matrix of the sheet-like breccia. Sandstones of this middle member, here termed "Pliocene sand drape," are unfossiliferous, pale yellowish-orange and grayish-orange, fine-grained, and are fairly well sorted. Grains are angular to subrounded. They drape over the "breccia beds" with dips ranging from 20 degrees southeast at the base, to essentially horizontal near the top of the beds. Well-lithified sandstone ledges, 1 to 8 cm thick, are cemented by calcium carbonate and may contain worm tube-like trace fossils, parting lineations, and small groove casts.

Pliocene sands are derived from local sandy Eocene carbonates. Petrographic studies of Pliocene sand show mineralogical and textural similarities to many Middle and Upper Eocene units. Southeastward depositional dips, cross-bedding that trends N135E, angular grains, and the presence of relatively unstable minerals, such as feldspars, micas, and hornblende, indicate a local source to the west or northwest.

Grayish-brown mudstone locally overlies the "breccia beds," especially between sections C and F. It is rich in bentonitic clays, never exceeds three meters, and usually lenses out north and south where it is exposed on the western flank of Gebel el-Rus.

Poorly lithified gravelly sandstones and sandy-pebbly conglomerates overlie the middle member sand and mudstone deposits. These form the upper member, here termed "Pliocene sandy and gravelly conglomerates" and contain numerous sandy, pebbly, and gravelly lenticular masses. Imbricated clasts (trending N135E), planar cross-bedding in sandy-pebbly lenses (trending N135E) and trough cross-bedding in sandy lenses (trending N125E) are characteristic of the ledge-forming conglomerates. No indigenous plant or animal fossils were found in Pliocene deposits on Gebel el-Rus; however, reworked Upper Eocene clams, oysters, and snails occur as second-cycle shells and shell fragments. Many clasts of Eocene sandstone and limestone contain Middle and Upper Eocene gastropods, clams and oysters.

Fragments of silicified wood, up to 1/2 m are present in these gravelly conglomerates, as are silicified burrows, usually less than 10 cm. Shell fragments, silicified wood and burrows together represent about one percent of these gravels. Rounded clasts of Eocene, chert, and quartzite make up the remaining 99 percent.

Facies Interpretation

Breccia lenses are the earliest Pliocene deposits in the area of study. They are interpreted as debris flows that have cut channels into upper Eocene strata, on "northern ridge," and into Middle Eocene strata on "western ridge" and "monkey ridge." They represent several events of subaerial mass wasting. Angularity, large size and distribution of clasts indicate the source to be Eocene cliffs and steep slopes to the west where the present-day Fayum depression lies.

Areas along both the west and east banks of the Nile valley had been dissected by streams before the beginning of the Pliocene. Messinian lowering of the Mediterranean Sea initiated entrenchment of the Nile which resulted in a deep Nile valley gorge. Deep erosion also dissected the northern Egyptian Eocene platform, including the Fayum region.

Breccias, like the "breccia beds" in the study area, are common in many locations along the Nile River valley.

According to Sanford and Arkell (1933: 1092), many coarse breccias occur to the south in the Thebaids on the Nile's west bank above Armant. Little (1935: 228) mapped many of these deposits along an ancient northern shoreline of the Pliocene Gulf. The present study confirms Little's observation that blocks often dip 5 degrees to 15 degrees toward the west and northwest. However, some blocks of the channeled debris flow deposits dip west 30 degrees to 50 degrees and the average orientation is best described as random.

According to Said (1981: 20), the position of the Nile River valley is controlled by tectonics and Gorshkov (1963: 101–105), notes that the valley has been the site of numerous major historic earthquakes. Said (1981: 21) suggested that movements of the "slipped masses," which accumulated at the foot of cliffs in the proto-Nile valley, were induced by earthquakes. However, modern slumps of Middle and Upper Eocene units on the flanks of the "northern and northeastern ridges" of Gebel el-Rus, have apparently been detached and accumulated by normal subaerial erosion processes. The writer proposes that ancient slumps may also have formed by the winnowing of erodible units below the slumped masses.

Little (1936, p. 228) described the source horizons for the ancient slumps and noted that they have since been eroded northward from 10 to 20 km. These source rocks formed Pliocene strike ridges subparallel to the modern Nile valley. Catastrophic debris flows, which likely resulted from flash floods, had potential to transport large blocks and erode deep channels.

"Breccia beds" of the study area most likely resulted from subaerial mass wasting and mud and debris flows beginning in early Pliocene. Aigner (1983: 118) suggested, however, that similar beds near Cairo resulted from wave erosion that accompanied the transgressing Pliocene gulf. He further proposed that detached blocks were deposited directly into the estuary. Little (1936: 228) hypothesized that many slumped block deposits scattered along the Nile River valley mark the ancient shoreline of the Pliocene gulf.

Channeled debris flow deposits at Gebel el-Rus are

terrestrial, not subaqueous. Many of the paleochannels slope from west to east, following the paleoslope into the gulf rather than paralleling its shoreline. The sheet-like slumped masses were probably detached like the modern debris accumulations on Gebel el-Rus and subsequently washed into channels.

The Pliocene sand and mud that overlies the "breccia beds" represent a fining-upward sequence deposited along the margins of the transgressing Pliocene gulf. Attitudes of the sandstone beds are due to the southeastward paleoslope and differential compaction of the water-saturated sediments over the irregular upper surface of the "breccia beds." These sands are too well sorted to be alluvial and grains are too angular and the deposits too muddy to be eolian. Occasional clayey mudstone lenses in the sand support the theory of marginal marine or estuarine deposits, and that they accumulated where the Pliocene gulf transgressed over at least some of the eastern Fayum.

Just as a fining-upward sequence indicates transgression of the Pliocene gulf, a subsequent coarsening-upward sequence marks its regression. The moderate dipping sand deposits grade upward into a horizontal sandstone which suggests flattening the paleoslope. Late Pliocene deposits are mostly pebbly and gravelly sandstones, sandy pebble conglomerates, and, at the top, coarse pebble to cobble conglomerates, as the gulf withdrew from the eastern Fayum.

Cliffs and steep slopes retreated northward in later Pliocene as the result of headward erosion of fluvial systems which emptied into the retreating gulf from the west and northwest. Sediments deposited in this environment are preserved near the summits and high ridges of Gebel el-Rus. These partially lithified sandstones, containing numerous pebble and gravel lenses and reworked Eocene gastropods and oyster and clam shells, are characteristic of a braided stream-alluvial fan complex. The source of these sands and gravels was Eocene sandstones in surrounding Pliocene cliffs. The later appearance of chert-dominated gravel lenses suggest fluvial systems energetic enough to transport coarse sediments from Oligocene rocks now preserved 30 km to the northwest.

Chert and quartzite clasts are likely from Oligocene interdeltaic and fluvial gravels. Said (1962: 103–104) described fluvial, estuarine, and marine gravels north of the Fayum. These sediments were transported and deposited by a proto-Nile River. The local source for cherty gravels on Gebel el-Rus is not known at the present. Quartzite clasts suggest a metamorphic source.

Gravelly conglomerates intercalated with the sandstone lenses, which outcrop near the peaks of Gebel el-Rus, probably accumulated in braided streams. Multiple scour-and-fill structures, poor sorting, planar cross-bedding, multiple-bidirectional low cross-bed sets, and imbricated clasts support this proposal. Paleocurrents ranged from N100E to N145E.

Pliocene-Eocene Contact in Unconformable Relationship

The angular Eocene-Pliocene contact is well exposed on the west and north flanks of Gebel el-Rus. The unconformity is accentuated by a distinct undulating erosional surface, especially evident along "northern ridge," and light Eocene rocks abutt darker Pliocene rocks in exposures between "western ridge" and "monkey ridge."

The unconformable relationship in the study area ranges from a disconformity to a minor angular unconformity. Angular discordance is most apparent north of "monkey ridge" on the west flank of "northern ridge." On the south side of "northern ridge" Eocene strata dip 5 degrees northwestward beneath horizontal ledge-forming Pliocene units. The angular relationship becomes readily apparent as the Eocene "*Ophiomorpha* sandstone" and "contact sandstone" are traced southeastward along "northern ridge." These units dip into the subsurface north of the study area but are truncated southeastward by Pliocene "breccia beds" between "northern ridge" and "western ridge." Angular discordance truncates the "western ridge sandstone," "graveyard limestone," and "orange limestone" northwest of Seila Pyramid.

Near "western ridge," the "western ridge sandstone"

is essentially horizontal; the unconformity becomes more angular southward between "western ridge" and "monkey ridge" and decreases again to a disconformity south of "monkey ridge."

A Geologic History in Summary

Most of Egypt was covered by the Tethys Sea during the Early Tertiary Cenomanian transgression. Paleocene and Lower Eocene sediments were deposited on an undulating surface of folded Cretaceous strata, thick deposits in structural basins and thin Lower Eocene sediments over anticlinal highs.

Minor gentle transgressive and regressive events in the Middle Eocene are recorded by gradual shifts of broad facies patterns in northern Egypt. Eocene strata in the study area correlate well with Eocene rocks throughout northern and central Egypt as part of a sheet of sediments uniformly deposited over that large region. Middle Eocene sediments of the Fayum and surrounding regions accumulated in open, shallow subtropical seas where tides influenced sedimentation (fig. 4a).

Seas regressed from northern Egypt during the Late Eocene and throughout the Oligocene. Upper Eocene littoral and tidal environments graded into Oligocene estuarine and fluvial conditions north of the Fayum depression. Progradation of terrestrial deposits accompanied withdrawal of the seas. Much of the Upper Eocene and all Oligocene and Miocene deposits are absent in the eastern Fayum, suggesting Mio-Pliocene erosion, and the region may have been subject to subaerial erosion from the beginning of the Oligocene.

Contemporaneous with the Late Eocene-Early Oligocene regression was gentle regional folding and faulting of older strata in northern Egypt. This diastrophic event was responsible for uplift of the Eocene platform. Basalt flows, which originally covered a large area between Cairo and the Fayum, were extruded during the Late Oligocene and Early Miocene. These volcanic events were apparently concurrent with uplift of pre-Miocene rocks north of the study area (fig. 4b).

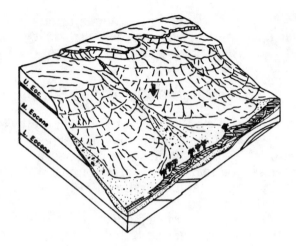

Figure 5. Generalized block diagram of the eastern Fayum region (Gebel el-Rus area) during the Late Miocene. The Nile River Valley and areas adjacent were heavily dissected due to a lower local base level during the Messinian desiccation of the Mediterranean Sea. Study area marked with an arrow.

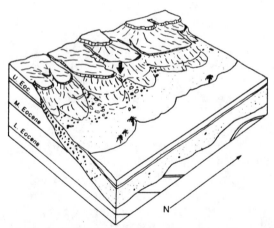

Figure 6. Generalized block diagram of the eastern Fayum region (Gebel el-Rus area) during the Early Pliocene. A transgressing gulf invaded the Nile Valley and part of the eastern Fayum. Study area is marked with an arrow.

Eocene strata of Gebel el-Rus were deposited on the stable part of the North African shelf but near the unstable part. Therefore, rocks in the Fayum area show only limited folding and only minor faults. Upper and Middle Eocene rocks in Gebel el-Rus generally dip north at 5 degrees to 10 degrees in a regional trend only locally interrupted by low anticlines and synclines.

The Eocene platform was extensively dissected during the Late Miocene. Erosion was strongly accelerated by steepened gradients produced by lowering the local base level thousands of feet when the Mediterranean Sea dried up during the Messinian. The Proto-Nile River reacted by eroding a deep, narrow gorge over 1300 km long. Pre-Pliocene rocks adjacent to this canyon and on the northern Egyptian platform were also deeply dissected (fig. 5).

The early Pliocene record begins in the Fayum area with debris flows, often confined to earlier channels. Where preserved, these beds delineate surface relief at the beginning of the Pliocene and also the paleoshoreline of a marine transgression. This Pliocene gulf is documented by a fining-upward sequence of sand and clayey muds deposited over the coarse debris flow deposits. The intensity and direction of the paleoslope is suggested by layering in the sands which dips from 5 degrees to 20 degrees toward the southeast. A coarsening-upward sequence of gravelly conglomerates was deposited over the sands and muds and represents coarse marginal debris as the Pliocene Gulf regressed from the study area. These later Pliocene braided stream-alluvial fan deposits transported and reworked older deltaic gravels from the northwest (fig. 6).

Steep slopes and cliffs at least as young as late Pliocene stood where the eastern side of the Fayum depression now lies, and since that time have been eroded back 25 or 40 km to the north. Paleochannels filled with debris flow deposits and braided stream paleochannels both show sediment transport from northwest to southeast out of a high source area now occupied by the Fayum depression.

Absence of Pliocene rocks in the Fayum oasis and the presence of Pliocene deposits rimming Nile-Fayum escarpments and derived from local western sources demonstrate that the Fayum depression, as we know it, did not exist during the Pliocene. The Pliocene gulf that occupied the Nile valley would likely have filled a nearby topographic low like the Fayum depression and at least some sedimentary record of it would have been preserved. The level of the gulf was at least 80 m above the present Nile river, as interpreted from the Pliocene clay deposits on Gebel el-Rus. Paleocurrents, documented by many sedimentary structures in the Pliocene deposits give strong evidence that sediments were transported from western and northwestern sources. The large size and angularity of blocks, derived from Eocene units and deposited in paleochannels, support the proposal that their source was nearby highlands that existed in the area where the depression presently lies. Pliocene rocks on Gebel el-Rus are from sources that no longer exist and were deposited on areas of low relief on slopes facing the Nile valley.

Excavation of at least the eastern part of the Fayum depression must have taken place subsequent to deposition of all Pliocene rocks on Gebel el-Rus, probably beginning in late Pliocene or early Pleistocene. The origin of the depression is unknown, however, it may be the result of a number of complex mechanisms, including regional subsidence due to minor faulting, erosion of minor structural features, intense mechanical erosion of thick unlithified mudstone units not overlain by resistant Pliocene "breccia bed" deposits and chemical erosion of limestone units when humid climatic conditions prevailed, and later subaerial wind erosion for final modification during arid Holocene times. Periods of glaciation during the Pleistocene, lowered global sea level hundreds of feet and additional removal of Eocene rocks from the Fayum depression probably resulted from erosive processes attendant to lower base level and wetter climate.

The Pleistocene was a significant epoch for the geomorphology of the Fayum region because, during this time, a major topographic reversal occurred. Gebel el-Rus and other highland areas along the eastern Fayum margin were low relief during the Pliocene. Valleys that sloped toward the deep proto-Nile gorge were filled with resistant debris flow and gravel deposits that became areas of high relief.   Source areas that once stood as a high platform with prominent eastward-facing cliffs were lowered by erosion to negative relief during the Pleistocene (fig. 7).

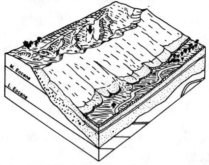

Figure 7. Generalized block diagram of the eastern Fayum region (Gebel el-Rus area) during late Pleistocene-Holocene times. A topographic reversal largely completed by this time produced a steep escarpment on the west side and gently inclined slope on the east side of the newly formed Nile-Fayum divide. The study area is marked with an arrow.

Natural excavation of the Fayum depression was essentially completed by the Paleolithic and lacustrine deposits dating from that time are preserved in the depression. Birket el-Qarun (Lake of Qarun) occupies the northern parts of the modern depression and is a remnant of ancient Lake Moeris that periodically covered the depression. Lake Moeris deposits are preserved on the lower western and southern slopes of Gebel el-Rus.

References

Aigner, Thomas. (1983). A Pliocene cliff-line around the Giza Pyramids Plateau, Egypt. Palaeogeography, Palaeoclimatology, Palaeoecology, 42, 313-22.

Beadnell, H. J. L. (1901). The Fayum depression: A preliminary notice of the geology of a district in Egypt containing a new paleogene fauna. Geological Magazine, 8 (Decade 4), 540-46.

Beadnell, H. J. L. (1905). The topography and geology of Fayum. Egypt Geological Survey, 101.

Blackenhorn, M. (1901). Geologic Aegyptens, Berlin 1901, (Part 4), 330-44.

Blackenhorn, M. (1902). Neue Geologisch-Stratigraph. Beobachtungen in Aegypten, S-Ber. d. Math-Physics. Classe d. Kgl. Bayer. Ac. d. Wiss. Bd. XXXI 1902, Heft III, Munchen 1902, 428-29.

Caton-Thompson, G., & Gardner, E. W. (1934). The desert Fayum. London: Royal Anthropological Institute.

Gardner, E. W. (1927). The recent geology of the northern Fayum Desert. J. Royal Anthropology Institute, 56, 301-308.

Gardner, E. W. (1929). The origin of the Fayum depression: A critical commentary on a new view of its origin. Geograph. J., 74, 371-83.

Gorshkov, G. P. (1963). The seismicity of Africa. A review of the natural resources of the African continent. UNESCO, Paris, 101-05.

Henson, F. R. S. (1951). Observations on the geology and petroleum occurences in the Middle East. Proc. Third World Petrol. Congr., Sec. I, 118-40.

Issawi, Bahay. (1972). Review of upper cretaceous-lower tertiary stratigraphy in central and southern Egypt. The American Association of Petroleum Geologists Bulletin, 56, 1448-63.

Little, O. H. (1936). Recent geological work in Fayum and adjoining portion of the Nile Valley. Bulletin Institute Egypt, 18, 201-40.

Said, Rushidi. (1961). Tectonic framework and its influence on distribution of Forminifera. The American Association of Petroleum Geologists Bulletin, 45, 198-218.

Said, Rushidi. (1962). The geology of Egypt. Amsterdam-New York: Elsevier.

Said, Rushidi. (1981). The geological evolution of the River Nile. New York: Springer-Verlag.

Salem, Rafik. (1976). Evolution of Eocene-Miocene sedimentation pattern in parts of Northern Egypt. The American Association of Petroleum Geologists Bulletin, 60, 34-64.

Sandford, K. S., & Arkell, W. J. (1928). The relations of Nile and Fayum in Pliocene and Pleistocene times [Letter to the editor]. Nature, 121, 670-71.

Sandford, K. S., & Arkell, W. J. (1933). Paleolithic man and the Nile Valley in Nubia, and Upper Egypt. Chicago University Oriental Inst. Publ., 17, 1-92.

Tamer, A., El-Shazly, M., & Shata, A. (1975). Geology of the Fayum-Beni Suef Region: Part II Geomorphology. Desert Institute Bulletin, 25(1-2), 17-25.

Tamer, A., El-Shazly, M., & Shata, A. (1975). Geology of the Fayum-Beni Suef Region: Part II Stratigraphy. Desert Institute Bulletin, 25(1-2), 27-45.

Excavating a Christian Cemetery Near Seila, in the Fayum Region of Egypt*   5

C. Wilfred Griggs

*M*ay I begin this report with an expression of gratitude to Dr. Ahmed Kadry, Dr. Ali Kholy, Mr. Mutawe Balboush, and other officers and members of the Egyptian Antiquities Organization, for generous interest and support for Brigham Young University in its excavation work at the site of Seila. The excavation staff members express heartfelt gratitude to the Mormon Archaeology and Research Foundation and its director, Mr. Wallace O. Tanner, and to Brigham Young University and its administrators for temporal and financial support for the Seila excavation project.

The archaeological site of Seila, taking its name from a nearby Egyptian village close to the eastern edge of the Fayum depression (see fig. 1, a map showing the site in relationship to the Fayum depression), is comprised of numerous components representing the entire scope of Egyptian history. Brigham Young University began work at the site in 1980, working jointly with the University of California at Berkeley that year, and having sole responsibility for the excavation since 1981.

* This report was delivered by Dr. C. Wilfred Griggs at the Third International Congress of Coptic Studies in Warsaw, Poland, 19–25 August 1984.

C. Wilfred Griggs is professor of ancient scripture and director of ancient studies in the Religious Studies Center at Brigham Young University.

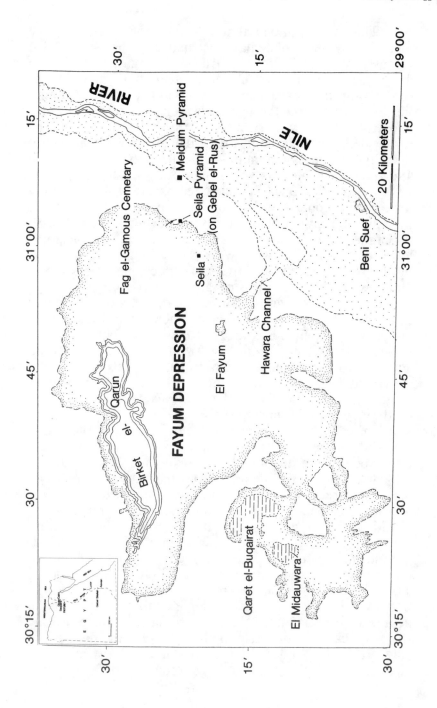

The oldest monument in the concession is the four-step pyramid of Seila constructed in the early Third Dynasty atop the Gebel el-Rus and situated on a line directly east of the 4th Dynasty Meidum pyramid. What relationship may exist between the later Meidum pyramid, the southernmost of the pyramids along the so-called Pyramid Row of the western edge of the Nile valley, and the earlier Seila pyramid, built on a ridge at the eastern edge of the Fayum depression and visible from both the Fayum and the Nile valley, is yet to be determined. During the 1981 season the BYU-Berkeley team removed the sandy debris from about one half of the exposed portion of the pyramid. Beneath the dust and sand accumulated over five millennia was a weathered and eroded surface, but some lower portions of the walls were protected from weathering by the aeolian sands, and there the limestone blocks are in quite good condition, measuring, on the average, 1 X 1/2 X 1/2 m. Much work yet remains to be done, both to uncover the pyramid totally and to place it accurately in the early historical and religious context of the Third Dynasty.

Approximately 2 km northwest of the pyramid and adjacent to the Abdallah Wahbi canal, which borders the cultivated land on the east of the Fayum, is an ancient cemetery which now bears the name Fag el-Gamous (Way of the Cow). A large limestone stele was erected on the western edge of the cemetery, not far from the canal (probably adjacent to the road leading south from Philadelphia, about 5 km north of the cemetery), and perhaps was intended to be an identification marker or dedicatory monument relating to the entire area. The stele is so badly weathered, however, that no markings remain on it which would assist in determining its function. The cemetery itself, covering approximately 300 acres (125 hectares), is almost entirely unplundered, though repeated digging for interment of bodies and later subsidence of the burial shafts have left the entire area in a very disturbed condition. A few very deep shafts, ranging from 15 to 23 m in depth, have horizontal shafts and burial chambers leading from the base of the vertical shafts, and these date probably from the Middle Kingdom. One unfinished burial chamber, beginning with a large room (c. 3x3 m) hewn from a limestone ridge running east-west in the cemetery continues north in a shaft for approximately 4–5 m before turning east in an unfinished burial chamber. Other rectangular shafts approximately one meter square and hewn into the small hills and mounds of the cemetery area angle downward and appear to turn horizontally left or right to burial chambers, but these have not yet been excavated, and firm dates cannot be assigned to them.

The BYU team has concentrated in an area of the cemetery which dates from the first century before the common era through the eighth century BCE, based on artifact analysis, including pottery, coins, textiles, and jewelry.

Within the portion of the cemetery excavated to the present time, two patterns of interment can be distinguished. The first consists of shafts hewn through the limestone bedrock to varying depths for burial. The most shallow are approximately one meter deep, into which were placed shrouded remains partially or wholly enclosed in wooden sarcophagi. Some of the shafts contained a narrower burial pit at the bottom, in which the burial was placed, and dressed rocks were placed over the body, resting on the rock shelves formed when the burial pit was cut into the base of the shaft. Gypsum plaster was then poured over the rocks, sealing the burial in its tomb. The shaft was then filled to ground level with rocks, sand, and miscellaneous debris and subsequently cemented by halite salt. Other shafts extended to a depth of as much as four m, then branched horizontally into burial chambers of varying sizes and degrees of sophistication in construction (i.e., with rooms, doorways with rock thresholds, and dressed, though undecorated, walls).

In all of the shaft burials hewn through the limestone bedrock, the decomposition of the remains and related organic artifacts was virtually complete. Sealing in the moisture and the atmosphere of the burial by means of the gypsum plaster caps prevented the desiccation of the body, and the artifact recovery from this portion of the cemetery has been limited to pottery, jewelry, and skeletal remains. A small amount of gold, including an amulet, two nuggets, and a gold-filled tooth, also came from burials in the rock-shaft tombs. Burials ranged in number from one in the shallow shafts to twelve in the deep shafts, with burial chambers branching off horizontally from the shaft. We cannot determine whether the large number of burials in one shaft-tomb represented a family burial, opened repeatedly as different members of the family died (both children and adults were buried in the multiple-burial tombs), or whether some catastrophe in the village or family resulted in a mass common burial effort.

After excavating some 17-shaft burial chambers, the team moved across a small wadi (approximately 100 m north) to excavate in an area comprised of aeolian sands, fanglomerates, lakeshore sands and gravels. Burials were encountered near the surface where some have been exposed and removed by erosion, and within the first 5 X 5 m area 22 bodies were recovered between the surface and the depth of 1.5 m. Because the normal factors of Egyptian desert geography and climate (sand and low humidity) played their roles in this region of the cemetery, the condition of recovered artifacts was considerably better than in the limestone shaft burials. In addition to pottery and jewelry, burial wrappings were often well-preserved, and textiles have been recovered in great abundance. During the 1981 season, the excavators recovered some mummiform burials which had articles of clothing neatly wrapped and placed on the face of the deceased. When the corpse was wrapped for burial, after being clothed in linen garments overlaid with an embroidered robe worn like a serape, the extra clothing on the face made the shrouded corpse appear deformed at the head. Of the 123 burials excavated in 100 square meters during the 1984 season, none had the extra clothing wrapped upon the face, although various articles of clothing were placed in close proximity to a body. There were, however, numerous burials which had linen or palm-fiber rope folded to many thicknesses or intertwined into woven designs and placed upon the face just as the articles of clothing were in some of the burials found in 1981. We are quite certain that this aspect of the burial technique found often in the cemetery has religious significance, but we have not yet ascertained its meaning. Many head coverings have been excavated, including a number of hooded robes associated with both males and females, children and adults. The quality of cloth ranges from very coarse material to finely-woven linen, and there are many samples of embroidered designs. Some designs are geometric and others are symbolic, including a design resembling the Egyptian *Wedjet eye* and some sacerdotal symbols, and there is also some representational art, including one piece of cloth adorned with brightly colored ducks. Some cloth is hemmed and other pieces have fringed edges, with some of the fringe up to 25 cm long. Most of the burials were wrapped with linen ribbon, averaging a little more than 1 cm in width, and containing simple geometric designs in red, black, or white. These ribbons were wrapped in geometric crisscrossing patterns over the shrouded body, often with numerous wraps about the feet and neck areas. Although there is much similarity in clothing and wrapping techniques, individual differences from body to body show that each family (or whoever assumed responsibility for burials) was free to modify slightly the general methods and customs.

The jewelry associated with the burials consists mostly of necklaces, bracelets, and earrings. The materials used in fabricating the pieces include copper, bronze, tin, silver, and a slight amount of gold, as mentioned before. There are also some ceramic bracelets, and a few necklaces and bracelets were made of polished semi-precious stones, held together by single-strand fiber twine or a fabric string. Wire clasps are common for all kinds of jewelry, and one pair of earrings consists of four pendant pearls on each earring, connected to a wire clasp for wearing in pierced earlobes. The jewelry is found mostly with female burials, both children and adults. The observations that most burials do not have jewelry associated with them, and that the artifacts are made from relatively inexpensive and commonly available materials (with a very few notable exceptions which, if anything, tend to emphasize the mean quality of the rest), lead us to the conclusion that burial jewelry in the excavated portion of the cemetery had a sentimental value for the families associated with burying the deceased, rather than religious or commercial value. This may be an argument for the generally low economic status of the people associated with the cemetery, but one may also suggest that religious beliefs precluded the necessity of burying much of worldly value with the dead. The quality and amount of textiles buried with many of the bodies demonstrates that care was taken to ensure that the deceased were properly prepared for interment, and if this world's goods were thought to be necessary in the post-mortal existence, more such artifacts would be expected to appear in the excavation.

Virtually all the burials in the cemetery are buried on an east-west axis, with variations that correspond to the sun's amplitude at different seasons of the year. The joint planes of the limestone bedrock happen to run in the same directions, and one could account for east-west burial shafts in that portion of the cemetery by assuming that it was easier to dig shafts along those joint fractures than across or against them. That supposition does not hold in the sandy areas of the cemetery, however, where digging grave shafts would have been equally easy in any direction, and the burials still fall on the east-west axis. We conclude, therefore, that direction of burial was important for reasons beyond those associated with ease of digging, and we further surmise that one might determine the season of digging the shaft by noting where on the sun's amplitude the axis falls. This would be valid only for the first burial in the shaft, since later burials would be added to the reopened shaft without attempting to align the body with the seasonal amplitude of the sun's rising. In the shafts dug in the sandy portion of the cemetery, there are as many as five burials from near the surface to the bottom of the shafts, each shaft having an average depth of about three m (see fig. 2, sketch illustrating burial patterns in the sandy portions of the cemetery). However, the burials are not evenly spaced in depth, but sometimes one touches the next above or below, and at other times the burial layers are a meter apart. In some instances children and adults are clustered, as if in family units; in other instances there seem to be no connections between burials in the same shaft. Bundles of reeds used as head markers, pottery, and other artifacts were placed as markers in strata well beneath the surface of the ground, where it would be impossible to see them after the shaft was filled. The reasons for

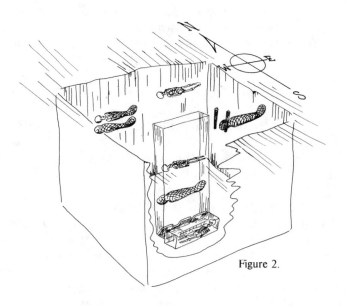

Figure 2.

placing such markers beneath the ground have not yet been determined. The burial technique for the first burial, at the bottom of the shaft, differed in most instances from the later (and higher) interments. Angling slightly to the north or south of the vertical shaft the diggers fashioned a burial chamber with dressed stones or mud bricks, often leaning them at an angle from the floor to the wall of the shaft. Only rarely did burials of the upper strata exhibit the same protective measures, and then large amphora shards were used as often as the dressed rocks or mud bricks. In addition to the added effort made for burials at the base of the shafts, one especially noteworthy difference from all other layers must be mentioned. *All* of the burials from upper layers were placed with the feet at the east and head at the west, suggesting that the person would arise in a resurrection facing east. The bottom layer burials, however, *almost always* reverse the direction, having the head to the east and feet to the west. Such a significant and total change of technique in one of the most conservative and pervasive ritual activities of man can best be accounted for by a major cultural upheaval in the area. Because the pottery of all strata above the bottom layer dates from the second century C.E. and later (the pottery is often mixed because of disturbances caused by reopening shafts), and because the pottery from the bottom layers of shafts dates from the first centuries BCE and C.E., we propose that the cultural change occurred around the end of the first century C.E. The discovery of two terra cotta figurines of robed figures, one complete and one broken (an angel, the Virgin Mary?) in the burial level just above the bottom of the shafts suggest the arrival and widespread adoption of Christianity. The late first century—early second century C.E. pottery associated with these burials, and a consistency in burial techniques from that level to the present *terminus ad quem* of the eighth century C.E. at the surface level of the cemetery, lead to the further suggestion that the cultural change which occurred in this area around the end of the first century or the early part of the second century was dominant for at least the next six or seven centuries. Of course this hypothesis must remain somewhat conjectural until inscribed materials or other similarly indisputable artifacts of early Christianity are recovered, but it is at present the best explanation for such a remarkable shift in burial direction, and it also accords with the fact that Christianity became the dominant religion in Egypt for the succeeding centuries. One would thus not expect another major change in burial techniques after the arrival of the Christian faith, and none occurs. The argument for an early arrival and spread of Christianity within Egypt can be made from literary sources, but this may well be one of the first archaeological sources to support that proposition.

As mentioned above, the team excavated 123 burials in 100 square meters during the 1984 season (some had to be left *in situ* until a future season because they were in the baulk between areas), and the pathology of the bodies done by the three palaeopathologists on the staff yielded considerable information regarding gender, age, stature, and general health. Cranial analysis, including palaeodontology, bone development, especially in the epiphyses of the humerus, femur, and tibia, and determination of pubic width, subpubic angle, and the presence or absence of a lateral recurve were among the field activities of the pathologists in determining anthropological data. Of the 123 burials, 8 were so close to the surface of the ground

and so badly preserved or so fragmentary that no meaningful data could be obtained from them. From the remaining
115, however, the following general observations can be pre-
sented:

Newborn–6 month infants	7
6–18 month infants	7
18–36 month children	1
3–6 year olds	16
6–9 year olds	7
9–15 year olds	4

Gender is virtually impossible to determine in the
children, but the excellent state of preservation of the
bodies allowed positive identification of two males in the
oldest group (nine to fifteen years).

In the adult population of the excavated areas, there
were 31 males and 42 females, totalling approximately 2/3
of the total number of excavated bodies.

15–25 years	4 males	13 females
25–35 years	11 males	17 females
35–40 years	7 males	5 females
40 plus	9 males	7 females

It appears from this sample that infant mortality was
about three times as high to the age of six (31 burials) as it
was between the ages of six and fifteen (11 burials), and
female mortality during the child-bearing years (fifteen to
thirty-five) was just double that of males of the same age
group (30 to 15). The difference in male and female mortality rates for those older than thirty-five years was negli-
gible (16 to 14), according to this sample. Of course,
further excavation in the cemetery will enhance or modify
these observations, but they are offered for the four random sample areas excavated in the cemetery.

Not all of the burials had preserved head and body
hair, but the characteristics of those which did are rather
striking. Eight of the adult males had facial hair, i.e
.mustaches and/or beards, and two of the adults had quite
curly hair. Four of the adult females had very long hair,
and 2 of those had the hair braided and the braids were
wrapped over the ears and around the back of the head. Of
the 37 adults whose hair was still preserved, the most interesting observation relates to the hair color. There were 4

redheads, 16 blondes, 12 with light or medium brown hair, and only 5 with dark brown or black hair. Of those whose hair was preserved 54% were blondes or redheads, and the percentage grows to 87% when light-brown hair color is added. Such a preponderance of light-colored hair was unexpected, and it will be interesting to see if this trait continues to be exhibited throughout the cemetery.

The palaeodontology gave considerable information and also raised some interesting questions. The teeth of the infants were still in the bone, as expected, and the development of both baby and permanent teeth was normal for most of the subadult population, with some anomalies such as missing or defective teeth occurring then as they do now. It is in the adult population that dental characteristics are the most telling. Of the 73 adults, 37 had significant periodontal disease, or deterioration of the gum, to the extent that many had lost most or even all of their teeth. Most of those same bodies had some buildup of calculus around the teeth, and both periodontal disease and calculus problems point to the fact that there was little or no practice of dental hygiene, either in dietary selection or by cleaning the teeth and gums. Interestingly, however, there were only 14 adults who had any measurable decay in existing teeth, and most of that decay was minimal, often only one cavity per person. This lack of decay suggests little sugar in the diet, among other possible reasons. Ten adults had extremely good teeth, mostly females, and further analysis must precede conclusions regarding the wide disparity in dental conditions of the adults. The same is true for attrition in the teeth, which ranges from little wear to attrition to the root tips. At present it does not seem adequate to assign the difference in wear patterns totally to dietary causes, such as sand in breads, etc. Some scientists have offered to help in this matter by performing an isotopic analysis of bone fragments in order to determine individual diets more certainly.

This brief survey of the BYU excavation of the Fag el-Gamous cemetery in the Fayum leaves many questions unasked and others unanswered, but as the excavation continues in succeeding seasons, the data gleaned from burials and artifacts will yield increased understanding concerning the Roman-Christian period of Egyptian history, especially in the Fayum.

Glossary

Aeolian Sands:	Sand laid down by atmospheric currents, or produced or eroded by the wind.
Alluvial:	Clay, silt, sand, gravel, or similar unconsolidated material deposited by a stream or running water.
Anomaly:	An irregularity or deviation from normal.
Anticline:	A fold, the core of which contains the stratigraphically older rocks; it is convex upward.
Argillaceous:	Contains an appreciable amount of clay.
Basaltic Pillow Lava:	A general term for those lavas displaying pillow structure and considered to have formed in a subaqueous environment.
Baulk (Balk):	A low ridge of earth that marks a boundary line.
Biotite:	A widely distributed and important rock-forming mineral of the mica group, generally black, dark brown, or dark green, and forms a constituent of crystalline rocks.
Bioturbated:	Sediment churned and stirred by organisms.
Brecciated:	Said of a rock structure marked by an accumulation of angular fragments, or of an ore texture showing mineral fragments without notable rounding.
Bruxism:	Grinding and clenching of the teeth while asleep.
Calcareous:	A substance that contains a considerable percentage of calcium carbonate.

Calcareous-Clastic:	A rock or sediment composed principally of broken fragments (in this case calcium carbonate) that are derived from preexisting rocks and that have been transported some distance from their place of origin.
Calculus:	A hard mineral-like deposit on teeth.
Caldera:	A large, basin shaped volcanic depression, more or less circular in form, the diameter of which is many times greater than that of the included vent or vents, no matter what the steepness of the walls or form of the floor.
Caries:	Tooth decay.
Cervical:	Pertaining to the neck or side of a tooth.
Chert:	A hard, extremely dense dull to semi-vitreous, cryphocrystalline sedimentary rock.
Concrescence:	Two teeth, hereditarily formed or fused together as one.
Continental Rifting:	The continents moving away from each other by the sea-floor spreading along a median ridge or rift, producing new oceanic areas between the continents.
Coquinas:	A limestone composed wholly or chiefly of mechanically sorted fossil debris that experienced abrasion and transport before reaching the depositional site and that is weakly to moderately cemented but not completely compacted and indurated.
Demographics:	Statistical study of a population.
Dental Abrasion:	Wear on the side of the teeth.
Dental Attrition:	Wear on the biting surface of the teeth.
Dentin:	The inner layer of tooth structure.

Diastrophic:	Describes all movement of the crust produced by Earth forces, including the formation of ocean basins, continents, plateaus, and mountain ranges.
Divergent Plate Boundaries:	Within the Plate Tectonic model, this is a boundary separating two diverging plates.
Echinoid:	Any echinozoan belonging to the class Echinoidea, characterized by a subspherical to modified spherical shape, interlocking calcareous plates, and by movable appendages; e.g. a *sea urchin.*
Enamel:	The hard outer layer of tooth structure.
Embayment:	A bay, either the deep indentation or recess of a shoreline, or the large body of water thus formed.
Epicontinental:	Pertaining to the continental shelf.
Epiphysis:	Tongue of an intrusion which isd etached from its source.
Estuarine:	Deposits formed in a river estuary.
Fanglomerates:	A conglomerate rock formed on an alluvial fan.
Fluviatile:	Geologists use the term for the results of river action and for river life.
Foraminifera:	Any protozoan belonging to the order Foraminiferida, commonly found in marine to brackish environments from the Cambrian to the present.
Fossiliferous:	A rock containing fossils.
Fusiform:	Shaped like a spindle or cigar, tapering toward each end from a swollen middle.
Geomorphological:	Related to the science that treats the general configuration of the Earth's surface.

Glauconite:	A dull-green, amorphous, and earthy or granular mineral of the mica group. It occurs abundantly in greensand, and seems to be forming in the marine environment at the present time; it is the most common sedimentary iron silicate and is found in marine sedimentary rocks from the Cambrian to the present. It is an indicator of very slow sedimentation.
Hornblende:	The commonest mineral of the amphibole group. It may contain potassium and appreciable fluorine. It is commonly black, dark green, or brown, and occurs in distinct monoclinic crystals or in columnar, fibrous, or granular forms.
Hummocky:	Said of topographic landforms when they are uneven.
In situ:	Rocks formed in place, lacking transportation.
Interdeltaic Facies:	Depositional environment associated with deltas.
Imbricated:	Said of overlapping patterns of particular object.
Labial:	Refers to the lips. In dental terminology; the front of a tooth.
Lacustrine Deposits:	Pertaining to, produced by, or formed in a lake or lakes.
Lamina Dura:	The hard outer layer on the surface of bone.
Lateral:	Said of the direction of extension of strata, measured at right angles to the vertical direction.
Lenticular:	Resembling a lens in shape, especially a double-convex lens. The term may be applied to a body of rock, to a sedimentary structure, to a geomorphologic feature, or to a mineral habit.

Lithology:	The description of rocks, on the basis of such characteristics as color, structures, mineralogic composition, and grain size.
Malocclusion:	An abnormal relationship of the upper to the lower teeth.
Margin Faults (Boundary Faults):	A descriptive term used in coal-mining geology for a fault along which there has been sufficient displacement to truncate the coal-bearing strata and thus bound the coalfield.
Marly:	Containing not less than 15% calcium carbonate and no more than 75% clay.
Massif:	A massive topographic and structural feature in an orogenic belt, commonly formed of rocks more rigid than those of its surroundings.
Metamorphic Gneisses:	Foliated rocks formed by regional metamorphism in which bands or lenticles of granular minerals alternate with bands and lenticles in which minerals having flaky or elongate prismatic habits predominate. Commonly feldspar and quartz-rich.
Micrite:	A descriptive term used for the semiopaque, crystalline, matrix of limestones (diameter of less than 4 microns), consisting of chemically precipitated carbonate mud, and interpreted as a lithified ooze.
Microcline:	A clear, white to light-gray, pale-yellow, brick-red, or green mineral of the alkali feldspar group.
Microsparite:	Limestone whose carbonate-mud matrix has recrystallized to microspar with a diameter ranging from 5 to 20 microns.

Monoclinal:	Describes a unit of strata that dips or flexes from the horizontal in one direction only, and is not part of an anticline or syncline. It is generally a large feature of gentle dip.
Muscovite:	A mineral of the mica group. It is usually colorless, whitish, or pale brown, and is a common mineral in metamorphic rocks, in most acid igneous rocks, and in many sedimentary rocks.
MYBP:	Million years before present.
Neogene:	An interval of time incorporating the Miocene and Pliocene of the Tertiary period. When the Tertiary is designated as an era, then the Neogene, together with the Paleogene, may be considered to be its two periods.
Neritic:	Pertaining to the ocean environment or depth zone between low-tide level and 100 fathoms; also pertaining to the organisms living in that environment.
Nummulite:	Any protozoan belonging to the order of Foranimiferida. Its stratigraphic range is Upper Cretaceous to present.
Occiput:	The back part of the skull.
Ophiolitic Suite:	The association of ultramafic rocks with coarse-grained gabbro, coarse-grained diabase, volcanic rock, and red radiolarian chert in the Tethyan mountain system.
Paleochannels:	Remnant of a stream channel cut in older rock and filled by the sediments of younger overlying rock.
Paleoecology:	The study of the relationships between organisms and their environments, the death of organisms, and their burial

and postburial history in the geologic past based on fossil faunas and floras and their stratigraphic position.

Paleo-pathology: The study of disease in ancient man.

Palynologist: A person who studies plants, pollen and spores.

Peridotites: A coarse-grained plutonic rock composed chiefly of olivine with or without other mafic minerals such as pyroxenes, amphiboles, or micas, and containing little or no feldspars.

Petrographic Analysis: Use of a petrographic microscope using polarized light and a revolving stage for analyzing rocks and minerals in thin sections.

Plagioclase: A group of triclinic feldspars of general formula.

Polycrystalline: Describing an aggregate of crystals so assembled as to appear as one crystal.

Recurve: A region produced by the successive landward extension of a spit (a finger-like extension of the beach).

Reefal: Pertaining to a reef and its integral parts, especially to the carbonate deposits in and adjacent to a reef.

Sessile Benthonic: Bottom dwelling marine life that is permanently attached to a substrate and that is not free to move about.

Silicified: A rock altered by the addition of silica.

Sparker Profiling: A specific type of geophysical survey to analyze subsurface geology.

Spreading Centers: Same as divergent boundary.

Stele: In a plant, the primary vascular structure of a stem or root, together with the tissues which may be enclosed.

Stratigraphy: The branch of geology that deals with the definition and description of major and minor natural divisions of rocks available for study in outcrop or from subsurface, and with the interpretation of their significance in geologic history.

Strike-Slip Transform Boundaries: Within the Plate Tectonic model, this is a boundary wherein two adjacent plates move horizontally side by side, e.g. the San Andreas Fault.

Subduction Margin: Within the Plate Tectonic model, this is a boundary wherein two adjacent plates are converging, one being forced down and below the other where it is compressed by melting.

Subduction Zone: An elongate region along which a crustal block descends relative to another crustal block.

Sublittoral: Said of that part of the littoral zone that is between low tide and a depth of about 100 m.

Suture Line: A line of union between skull bones.

Synclines: A fold, the core of which contains the stratigraphically younger rocks; it is concave upward.

Tectonic: Said of or pertaining to the forces involved in, or the resulting structures or features of tectonics.

Terrestrial Vertebrates: Land dwelling vertebrate organism.

Terrigenous Deposits: Shallow marine sediments consisting of material eroded from the land surface.

Travertine: A hard, dense, finely crystalline, compact or massive but often concretionary limestone, of white, tan, or cream color, often having a fibrous or concentric structure and splintery fracture, formed by rapid chemical precipitation of calcium carbonate from solution in surface and ground waters.

Turritelled Gastropods:	A type of fossil gastropod similar to the genus Turritella.
Wackestones:	Mud-supported carbonate sedimentary rocks containing more than 10% grains (particles with diameters greater than 20 microns).
Wormian Sutures:	Quite irregular skull lines of union.